A SHAKESPEARE ANTHOLOGY

WILLIAM SHAKESPEARE
1564-1616

A SHAKESPEARE ANTHOLOGY

Selections from the Comedies, Histories, Tragedies, Songs and Sonnets, with an Introduction by

G. F. MAINE

COLLINS
LONDON AND GLASGOW

COLLINS GREETINGS BOOKS

General Editor: G. F. Maine

Titles in Collins Greetings Books

A SHAKESPEARE ANTHOLOGY
THE RUBÁIYÁT OF OMAR KHÁYYAM
THE GREATEST THING IN THE WORLD
MY LADY OF THE CHIMNEY CORNER
THE ROADMENDER
A WORDSWORTH ANTHOLOGY
LYRICS FROM THE GILBERT AND SULLIVAN OPERAS
A BOOK OF DAILY READINGS
THE LIFE AND TEACHINGS OF CHRIST
AN OPEN-AIR ANTHOLOGY
AS A MAN THINKETH
A DICKENS ANTHOLOGY
CHURCHILL: HIS WIT AND WISDOM
STREAMLINED THOUGHTS

Printed in Great Britain by
COLLINS CLEAR-TYPE PRESS

CONTENTS

INTRODUCTION

THE MAN SHAKESPEARE is an enigma. The documents relevant to the life and work of Shakespeare have been described as a Chinese puzzle in which some of the pieces are undecipherable scraps and several of the most important pieces missing. " No letter of his handwriting, no record of his conversation, no character of him drawn with any fulness by any contemporary has been produced," wrote Henry Hallam. True, it is now claimed by some that 147 lines of the manuscript Play of Sir Thomas More in the British Museum are in Shakespeare's handwriting, but experts are divided as to the identity of the hand. Of Shakespeare of Stratford it may truly be said that hardly anything is known. No one has succeeded in making a reliable chronology nor in shaping with firmness his elusive personality. The real Shakespeare is concealed in his works. There alone are to be found the exuberant genius, the deep psychological insight, the beauty and imagery of his poetic imagination.

His father, John Shakespeare, who was a devout

Catholic, established himself as a glover in Stratford about 1551. His venture was successful and in 1557 he married Mary Arden, only daughter of Robert Arden of Wilmecote. She, though an heiress to money and properties, was a simple country girl probably unable to read, certainly unable to write, yet her family, though it had fallen upon evil days, was "one of the noblest and oldest in Warwickshire." John Shakespeare's business continued to expand, and in addition to glove-making he would seem to have dealt in corn and hides, to have trafficked in wood and wool and traded as a butcher.

He also interested himself in town affairs and held in succession various municipal offices including that of Chamberlain, yet it seems improbable that he could read and he signed his name with a mark which may still be seen in the Chamberlain's accounts. In 1569 he was elected High Bailiff or Mayor of Stratford. He had risen from tenant farmer through the rank of yeoman to that of "gentleman," and when in 1575 he purchased the property in which he resided in Henley Street, this was the high-water mark of his prosperity. Now his fortunes began to ebb, and in 1586 a distress was issued against his goods. In March, 1587, he was imprisoned and sued out a writ of *habeas corpus* to obtain his liberty and in the same year he mortgaged the Asbies property, which his wife had inherited from her father, for £40, a transaction which he endeavoured in 1589, and again in 1597, to set aside, but without success. A year or two later he sold his interest in his Snitterfield property for £4, but in spite of these reverses he would seem steadily to have maintained his title and estate.

John Shakespeare had ten children of whom William was probably born on April 22nd or 23d, 1564. The birth is not recorded but the baptism took place on April 26th. Here we enter the region of probabilities. Nothing is known of Shakespeare's boyhood but there can be little doubt that he went for some years to the Free Grammar School of Stratford, the repair of which his father had sponsored during his tenure of office. The course of instruction may be conjectured from the customs of contemporary schools. It included reading and writing, but the stress was on Latin, then current throughout Europe as the language of culture and diplomacy. The Stratford scholars were taught from Virgil, Ovid, Horace, Plautus, etc., and the school possessed a copy of Cooper's *Thesaurus*. English was little taught in such schools ; the first English Grammar was not published until 1586. Was Shakespeare, perhaps in the year 1577 when he was thirteen, withdrawn from school before he had completed the usual curriculum and set to assist his father? There is no evidence that the boy was studious; we know nothing of what he knew, or thought or did at this period.

In 1582, when eighteen, Shakespeare had formed an intimacy with a neighbouring farmer's daughter, Anne Hathaway, some seven or eight years his senior, and a marriage ceremony took place in the church of Luddington on November 28th, 1582. Shakespeare's parents were averse to the marriage and, to hurry it on, two friends of Anne's father (who had lately died) took the unusual step of giving a bond in the Worcester registry on the 28th of November, 1582, which enabled it to be solemnised with one proclamation of banns. On the previous day the same registry had issued a licence for the marriage of William Shakspere with Ann Whately! Can it be that but for the action of her friends Shakespeare would have deserted Anne Hathaway and married another woman?

Shakespeare's daughter Susanna was baptised at Stratford on May 26th, 1583, and on February 2nd, 1585, the twins Hamnet and Judith were baptized. Thus before he had reached his twenty-first year Shakespeare had to support a wife and a family of three children. He is thought to have made his way to London about 1586 and there to have found employment in connection with a theatre. One theory is that he may have joined an itinerant company of players passing through Stratford and moved with them from place to place until, with the approach of winter, they betook themselves to their London headquarters.

In the sixteenth century the stage enjoyed the patronage of the court and a large section of the people. Its persistent enemies were Puritans in general, and, more particularly, the Common Council of London, which had long looked upon public shows as public nuisances, and which, had it possessed the power, would have quickly stamped out professional acting. Queen Elizabeth directly encouraged theatrical performances. For some years she had a company of the best actors in her service, and many of her nobles were patrons of other companies. Every Christmas dramatic performances were given before her, and in order that the players should be practised in their parts for these festivities the court frequently intervened in disputes between the magistrates of London and the much-threatened actors.

In 1578 a compromise was effected between the magistrates and the actors' friends at court. Six special companies were allowed to play in the city, that they might be perfect in their parts when they appeared before the Queen. Two such companies were made up of boys of the choirs of the Chapel Royal and of St. Paul's.

Singularly enough it was the endeavour of the Common Council to suppress plays that led to the erection of permanent theatres. About 1576 James Burbage, joiner, tavern-keeper, horse-hirer, actor, etc., adapted for stage performances a house in the precinct and liberty of Blackfriars, almost in the heart of the city, yet beyond the jurisdiction of the Lord Mayor and aldermen. About the same time Burbage built two other wooden buildings in Shoreditch, the Theatre and the Curtain, also outwith the reach of the London authorities.

Public theatrical performances were generally given in the daytime, so that during the winter months in London a large part of the evening was still at the disposal of the theatre-goer. It seems to have been the custom for gallants and those of literary tastes to invite the principal actors to supper at some ordinary :

"for some few crowns
Spent on a supper any man may be
Acquainted with them from their kings to clowns."

Out of gatherings such as these sprang the Mermaid Club, which held its meetings usually at the Falcon

Tavern, close to the Globe Theatre in Bankside. Among those known to have frequented this resort were Sir Walter Raleigh, Shakespeare, Jonson, Fletcher, and Beaumont, who has left a poetical description of the contests of wit that took place among the members.

In spite of long and patient investigation by scholars little is known of Shakespeare's life in London, and the first reference to any of his works is the production of the first part of King Henry the Sixth ("Harry the Sixth") in March, 1592, at Southwark or Newington Butts. In 1593 the plague raged in London and the theatres were closed, but it was in that year that there appeared Shakespeare's first publication *Venus and Adonis*, "imprinted by Richard Field, and are to be sold at the sign of the White Greyhound in Paule's Church-yard." In January, 1594, the Earl of Sussex's servants enacted *Titus Andronicus* at the Southwark theatre. This play was printed in 1594, 1600 and 1611, but no copy of the first edition has yet been discovered.

A writ of attachment issued by William Gardiner, High Sheriff of Surrey and Sussex, returnable on the eighteenth of St. Martin, i.e. November 29th, 1596, in which William Wayte craved sureties against William Shakespeare, Francis Langley, and others for fear of death and so forth, confirms that while in the Spring of 1596, the year of his son Hamnet's death, Shakespeare resided in the parish of St. Helen's, Bishopgate, in November of that year he was living in the Bailiwick of the Sheriff of Surrey. Gardiner, who was reputed a very mean sort of scoundrel, had threatened Langley, and Gardiner's stepson Wayte had in turn been threatened by Shakespeare and Langley. The year before, Langley had built his theatre, the Swan, in his Paris garden adjoining the Southwark Bankside. It is not known which company of players used this theatre prior to Pembroke's men in 1597. Could it have been that of which Shakespeare was a member, the which may have crossed the river to escape the bitter Puritan hostility of the time? And may not its repertoire have included the earlier version of *Hamlet*?

Shakespeare's company acted successively at the Theatre and the Curtain, both near Shoreditch, and at the Rose, the Globe and Blackfriars theatres. At Christmas, 1598, the players gave three performances before the Queen at Whitehall, and on December 26th they played at Richmond Palace. In 1599 the Globe Theatre was rebuilt in Southwark, close to the Bear Garden, out of the materials of the Theatre at Shoreditch, which the magistrates had at last succeeded in pulling down.

Every Man out of his Humour was the opening piece.

Shakespeare returned to Stratford in 1596 and in 1597 he purchased from William Underhill of Idlicote, Warwickshire, for £60, "New Place," the finest house but one in Stratford and thereafter spent part of his time there with his family and part in London until his final retirement to Stratford in 1611. In 1599 or 1600 he acquired from Richard Burbage and his brother shares in the new Globe and Blackfriars theatres which must have brought him a substantial income. The fact that his name does not appear in any acting list later than that of Jonson's *Sejanus*, first performed in 1603, is an indication that he retired from the stage soon afterwards.

Queen Elizabeth died on March 24th, 1603, having bequeathed the succession to James VI of Scotland. The new sovereign arrived in London on May 7th, and the actors ceased playing until their licence was renewed by royal authority. A few days after the king's arrival a licence was granted to "Laurence Fletcher, Wm. Shakespeare, and others." The fame of the Lord Chamberlain's players had reached James's ears before he left Scotland, and he lost no time in appointing these nine players to be "His Majesty's servants," with an annual fee of £3 6s. 8d. each. The king made his public entry into London on March 15th, 1604, and the players formed part of the royal procession.

With the accession of James the fear of civil war was lifted from the hearts of Englishmen, and the ban on English history was removed. Now there was no need for discretion and adroitness, and the resultant political and intellectual emancipation is mirrored in such plays as *Julius Cæsar* and *Troilus*, which, with *Hamlet*, *Pericles* and *Lear*, were the only new plays to be printed until 1623.

That Shakespeare was a shrewd man of business is evident in all his transactions, and also that he was not over-scrupulous. In a time of dearth when the poor stood to suffer grievously, he (in company with several of his most substantial and reputable neighbours) broke the law by " engrossing and forestalling " grain—and was very properly dealt with.

In January, 1616, Shakespeare instructed Francis Collins of Warwick to draft his will, and appointed as his executors Dr. John Hall and his daughter Susanna Hall. Next to these he appointed as overseers Francis Collins and Thomas Russell. It is plain that Shakespeare's desire was to found a family of gentlefolk on the basis of landed estate. His earnings were ample for the purpose but this ambition was doomed to failure. His male descendants all died in childhood and even the female line presently became extinct. On

February 10th his daughter Judith was married to Thomas Quiney, a vintner, the son of an old friend. The marriage was performed without a licence, and the ecclesiastical court of Worcester summoned the pair before it, and, after threatening them with excommunication, imposed a fine.

A few weeks later Shakespeare was suddenly taken ill. The nature of his disease is unknown, but that the prognosis was grave is plain from the fact that on March 10th the draft of the will, with an addition of some interlineations, was made to serve as the formal document. He died on April 23rd, and, on the 25th, his body was carried under the limes to the church of the Holy Trinity, and buried in the chapel in front of the altar. The stone over the grave bears the words :

> " Good frend, for Iesvs sake forbeare,
> to digg the dvst encloased heare ;
> Bleste be ye man yt spares thes stones,
> And curst be he yt moves my bones."

A few years after his death a monument in the form of a bust was executed by the Dutch sculptor Gerald Johnson and placed against the north wall of the church. An engraving of this may be seen in Sir William Dugdale's *Warwickshire* published in 1656. The present bust, which bears little resemblance to the other, was erected according to a resolution of a Stratford Committee of November, 1748. Below the bust is the inscription :

IVDICIO PYLIVM GENIO SOCRATEM ARTE MARONEM
TERRA TEGIT POPVLVS MÆRET OLYMPVS HABET
STAY PASSENGER WHY GOEST THOV BY SO FAST
READ IF THOV CANST WHOM ENVIOVS DEATH HATH PLAST
WITH IN THIS MONVMENT SHAKSPEARE WITH WHOME
QVICK NATVRE DIDE WHOSE NAME DOTH DECK Y TOMBE
FAR MORE THEN COST : SITH ALL YT HE HATH WRITT
LEAVES LIVING ART BVT PAGE TO SERVE HIS WITT

OBIIT ANO DO' 1616
ÆTATIS 53 DIE 23 AP

The controversy about the authorship, origins, order and meaning of the Plays, which has raged for more than three centuries, and which rises phœnix-like from its own ashes, is not one whit less vehement and voluble in the sphere of the Sonnets, about which diversity of opinion seems inexhaustible. Were the poems first published in 1609 or 1625? Do they appear in their correct order? Who was the poet's friend—Southampton or Pembroke or Powys or none of these? Were some of the Sonnets written to a man and some to a woman? Who was the " Dark Lady ? " For our own peace of mind perhaps we should follow the example of Gerald Bullett and dismiss their manifold enigmae in two sentences : " Whether historical personages are represented in these figures is not known, despite the conjectures of the learned. And who cares ? "

But whatever we decide the conjectures will go on ; there is a feeling that the last word has not yet been said, that at any moment some startling secret may come to light. The answer of the Baconians is that the mystery is solved ; that by virtue of a secret marriage to Leicester, Francis Bacon and Essex were Elizabeth's sons, and that if the Sonnets are read in a certain sequence they will be found to reveal the personal history of Bacon and confirm that he is the real Shakespeare.

And what of that sphinxlike poem of the glorification of spiritual love, *The Phoenix and the Turtle*, on which hundreds of scholars have cudgelled their brains and for a reasonable solution of which Ralph Waldo Emerson suggested that a prize be awarded ? Here in poetic language is a mystery which is perhaps quite incommunicable, that far transcends the arid interpertations of scholars. The poem is integrated by the controlling mind and purpose of a master, the rare expression of an experience of the soul which we may guess at but never fully comprehend. " Love hath reason reason none."

May it not be that we must learn to distinguish between two very different personalities, Shakspere and Shake-speare? The former is the shrewd man of business whose will, so full and meticulous in other particulars, makes reference to neither books nor manuscripts nor literary property. The other is the genius whose face is hidden but whose identity is revealed by a mind that bestrides the world like a Colossus.

There are in existence more than one hundred and sixty documents having a bearing upon Shakespeare's life, yet only a very few incidents have been authenticated; the rest is conjecture, supposition, indirect evidence, gossip, legend and the like. But if the man Shakespeare is an enigma, the literature which we call Shakespearian is perennial and dateless. As often as we return to it we experience anew the wonder of its beauty, its wisdom, its universality. It "throws down all barriers of centuries and schools" and makes us one with its imperishable reality.

G. F. MAINE

ARIEL'S SONG

Come unto these yellow sands,
  And then take hands :
Curtsied when you have, and kiss'd,
  The wild waves whist,
Foot it featly here and there ;
And, sweet sprites, the burden bear.
    Hark, hark !
        Bow, wow,
    The watch-dogs bark :
        Bow, wow,
    Hark, hark ! I hear
The strain of strutting Chanticleer
  Cry, Cock-a-diddle-dow.

Act I, Sc. 2.

SEA DIRGE

Full fathom five thy father lies :
    Of his bones are coral made ;
Those are pearls that were his eyes :
    Nothing of him that doth fade,
But doth suffer a sea-change
Into something rich and strange.
Sea-nymphs hourly ring his knell :
  Hark ! now I hear them,—
    Ding, dong, bell.

Act 1, Sc. 2.

SONG

Where the bee sucks, there suck I ;
In a cowslip's bell I lie :
There I couch when owls do cry.
On the bat's back I do fly
After summer merrily :
Merrily, merrily shall I live now,
Under the blossom that hangs on the bough.

Act 5, Sc. 1.

CELESTIAL MUSIC

Be not afeard : the isle is full of noises,
Sounds and sweet airs, that give delight, and
hurt not.
Sometimes a thousand twangling instruments
Will hum about mine ears ; and sometime
voices,
That, if I then had wak'd after long sleep,
Will make me sleep again : and then, in
dreaming,
The clouds methought would open and show
riches
Ready to drop upon me ; that, when I wak'd
I cried to dream again.

Act 3, Sc. 2.

THE STUFF OF DREAMS

Be cheerful, sir :
Our revels now are ended. These our actors,
As I foretold you, were all spirits and
Are melted into air, into thin air :
And, like the baseless fabric of this vision,
The cloud-capp'd towers, the gorgeous palaces.
The solemn temples, the great globe itself,
Yea, all which it inherit, shall dissolve
And, like this insubstantial pageant faded,
Leave not a rack behind. We are such stuff
As dreams are made on, and our little life
Is rounded with a sleep.

Act 4, Sc. 1.

THE ART OF MAGIC

Ye elves of hills, brooks, standing lakes, and groves;
And ye, that on the sands with printless foot
Do chase the ebbing Neptune and do fly him
When he comes back; you demi-puppets, that
By moonshine do the green sour ringlets make
Whereof the ewe not bites; and you, whose pastime
Is to make midnight mushrooms; that rejoice
To hear the solemn curfew; by whose aid,—
Weak masters though ye be—I have bedimm'd
The noontide sun, call'd forth the mutinous winds,
And 'twixt the green sea and the azur'd vault
Set roaring war: to the dread-rattling thunder
Have I given fire and rifted Jove's stout oak
With his own bolt: the strong-bas'd promontory
Have I made shake; and by the spurs pluck'd up
The pine and cedar: graves at my command
Have wak'd their sleepers, op'd, and let them forth
By my so potent art.

Act 5, Sc. 1.

CAPRICIOUS LOVE

O! how this spring of love resembleth
The uncertain glory of an April day,
Which now shows all the beauty of the sun,
And by and by a cloud takes all away!

Act 1, Sc. 3.

THE POWER OF POETRY

Say that upon the altar of her beauty
You sacrifice your tears, your sighs, your heart.
Write till your ink be dry, and with your tears
Moist it again, and frame some feeling line
That may discover such integrity:
For Orpheus' lute was strung with poets' sinews,
Whose golden touch could soften steel and stones,
Make tigers tame and huge leviathans
Forsake unsounded deeps to dance on sands.

Act 3, Sc. 2.

DIDST THOU BUT KNOW

Didst thou but know the inly touch of love,
Thou wouldst as soon go kindle fire with snow
As seek to quench the fire of love with words.
Lucetta. I do not seek to quench your love's hot fire,
But qualify the fire's extreme rage,
Lest it should burn above the bounds of reason.
Julia. The more thou damm'st it up, the more it burns.
The current that with gentle murmur glides,
Thou know'st, being stopp'd, impatiently doth rage ;
But when his fair course is not hindered,
He makes sweet music with th' enamell'd stones,
Giving a gentle kiss to every sedge
He overtaketh in his pilgrimage ;
And so by many winding nooks he strays
With willing sport, to the wild ocean.
Then let me go and hinder not my course :
I'll be as patient as a gentle stream
And make a pastime of each weary step,
Till the last step have brought me to my love ;
And there I'll rest, as after much turmoil
A blessed soul doth in Elysium.

Act 2, Sc. 7.

A LOVER'S BANISHMENT

And why not death rather than living torment?
To die is to be banish'd from myself;
And Silvia is myself: banish'd from her
Is self from self,—a deadly banishment!
What light is light, if Silvia be not seen?
What joy is joy, if Silvia be not by?
Unless it be to think that she is by
And feed upon the shadow of perfection.
Except I be by Silvia in the night,
There is no music in the nightingale;
Unless I look on Silvia in the day,
There is no day for me to look upon.

Act 3, Sc. 1.

SILVIA

Who is Silvia? What is she,
That all our swains commend her?
Holy, fair, and wise is she;
The heaven such grace did lend her,
That she might admirèd be.

Is she kind as she is fair?
For beauty lives with kindness.
Love doth to her eyes repair,
To help him of his blindness;
And, being helped, inhabits there

Then to Silvia let us sing,
That Silvia is excelling;
She excels each mortal thing,
Upon the dull earth dwelling:
To her let us garlands bring.

Act 4, Sc. 2.

ABUSE OF AUTHORITY

O! it is excellent
To have a giant's strength, but it is tyrannous
To use it like a giant. . . .
Could great men thunder
As Jove himself does, Jove would ne'er be quiet,
For every pelting, petty officer
Would use his heaven for thunder; nothing
but thunder.
Merciful heaven!
Thou rather with thy sharp and sulphurous bolt
Split'st the unwedgeable and gnarled oak
Than the soft myrtle; but man, proud man,
Drest in a little brief authority,
Most ignorant of what he's most assur'd,
His glassy essence, like an angry ape,
Plays such fantastic tricks before high heaven
As make the angels weep; who, with our
spleens,
Would all themselves laugh mortal.

Act 2, Sc. 2.

JUSTICE

He who the sword of heaven will bear
Should be as holy as severe ;
Pattern in himself to know,
Grace to stand, and virtue go ;
More nor less to others paying
Than by self offences weighing.
Shame to him whose cruel striking
Kills for faults of his own liking !
Twice treble shame on Angelo,
To weed my vice and let his grow !
O, what may man within him hide,
Though angel on the outward side !
How many likeness made in crimes,
Making practice on the times,
To draw with idle spiders' strings
Most pond'rous and substantial things !

Act 3, Sc. 2.

SEALS OF LOVE

Take, O take those lips away
That so sweetly were forsworn,
And those eyes, the break of day,
Lights that do mislead the morn.
But my kisses bring again,
    Bring again—
Seals of love, but sealed in vain,
    Sealed in vain !

Hide, oh hide those hills of snow,
Which thy frozen bosom bears,
On whose tops the pinks that grow
Are of those that April wears :
But my poor heart first set free,
Bound in those icy chains by thee.

Act 4, Sc. 1.

MAN'S PRE-EMINENCE

There's nothing situate under heaven's eye
But hath his bound, in earth, in sea, in sky:
The beasts, the fishes, and the winged fowls,
Are their males' subjects and at their controls.
Men, more divine, the masters of all these,
Lords of the wide world, and wild wat'ry seas,
Indu'd with intellectual sense and souls,
Of more pre-eminence than fish and fowls,
Are masters to their females and their lords:
Then, let your will attend on their accords.

Act 2, Sc. 1.

DEFAMATION

I see, the jewel best enamelled
Will lose his beauty ; and though gold bides still
That others touch, yet often touching will
Wear gold ; and no man that hath a name,
By falsehood and corruption doth it shame.

Act 2, Sc. I.

PATIENCE

Patience unmov'd ! no marvel though she pause ;
They can be meek that have no other cause.
A wretched soul, bruis'd with adversity,
We bid be quiet when we hear it cry ;
But were we burden'd with like weight of pain,
As much, or more we should ourselves complain.

Act 2, Sc. I.

LOVE OVERRIDES FRIENDSHIP

Friendship is constant in all other things
Save in the office and affairs of love :
Therefore all hearts in love use their own
tongues ;
Let every eye negotiate for itself
And trust no agent ; for beauty is a witch
Against whose charms faith melteth into blood.

Act 2, Sc. 1.

THE FRAUD OF MEN

Sigh no more, ladies, sigh no more ;
  Men were deceivers ever ;
One foot in sea, and one on shore,
  To one thing constant never :
Then sigh not so, but let them go,
  And be you blithe and bonny,
Converting all your sounds of woe
  Into Hey nonny, nonny.

Sing no more ditties, sing no moe,
  Of dumps so dull and heavy ;
The fraud of men was ever so,
Since summer first was leavy :
Then sigh not so, but let them go,
  And be you blithe and bonny,
Converting all your sounds of woe
  Into Hey nonny, nonny.

Act 2, Sc. 3.

VALUE OF THINGS LOST

But not for that dream I on this strange course.
But on this travail look for greater birth.
She dying, as it must be so maintain'd,
Upon the instant that she was accus'd,
Shall be lamented, pitied and excus'd
Of every hearer ; for it so falls out
That what we have we prize not to the worth
Whiles we enjoy it, but being lack'd and lost,
Why, then we rack the value, then we find
The virtue that possession would not show us
Whiles it was ours. So will it fare with Claudio :
When he shall hear she died upon his words,
The idea of her life shall sweetly creep
Into his study of imagination,
And every lovely organ of her life
Shall come apparell'd in more precious habit,
More moving-delicate, and full of life
Into the eye and prospect of his soul,
Than when she liv'd indeed.

Act 4, Sc. 1.

WOMEN'S EYES

From women's eyes this doctrine I derive :
They are the ground, the books, the academes,
From whence doth spring the true Promethean
fire.
Why, universal plodding poisons up
The nimble spirits in the arteries,
As motion and long-during action tires
The sinewy vigour of the traveller.
Now, for not looking on a woman's face,
You have in that forsworn the use of eyes,
And study too, the causer of your vow ;
For where is any author in the world
Teaches such beauty as a woman's eye ?
Learning is but an adjunct to ourself,
And where we are our learning likewise is :
Then when ourselves we see in ladies' eyes,
Do we not likewise see our learning there ?
O ! we have made a vow to study, lords,
And in that vow we have forsworn our books :
For when would you, my liege, or you, or you,
In leaden contemplation have found out
Such fiery numbers as the prompting eyes
Of beauty's tutors have enrich'd you with ?

Act 4, Sc. 3.

SONG

On a day, alack the day!
Love, whose month is ever May,
Spied a blossom passing fair
Playing in the wanton air:
Through the velvet leaves the wind,
All unseen, 'gan passage find;
That the lover, sick to death,
Wish'd himself the heaven's breath.
Air, quoth he, thy cheeks may blow;
Air, would I might triumph so!
But alack! my hand is sworn
Ne'er to pluck thee from thy thorn:
Vow, alack! for youth unmeet,
Youth so apt to pluck a sweet.
Do not call it sin in me,
That I am forsworn for thee;
Thou for whom e'en Jove would swear
Juno but an Ethiop were;
And deny himself for Jove,
Turning mortal for thy love.

Act 4, Sc. 3.

THE POWER OF LOVE

But love, first learned in a lady's eyes,
Lives not alone immured in the brain,
But, with the motion of all elements,
Courses as swift as thought in every power,
And gives to every power a double power,
Above their functions and their offices.
It adds a precious seeing to the eye ;
A lover's eyes will gaze an eagle blind ;
A lover's ear will hear the lowest sound,
When the suspicious head of theft is stopp'd :
Love's feeling is more soft and sensible
Than are the tender horns of cockled snails :
Love's tongue proves dainty Bacchus gross in
taste.
For valour, is not Love a Hercules,
Still climbing trees in the Hesperides ?
Subtle as Sphinx ; as sweet and musical
As bright Apollo's lute, strung with his hair ;
And when Love speaks, the voice of all the gods
Makes heaven drowsy with the harmony.
Never durst poet touch a pen to write
Until his ink were temper'd with Love's sighs ;
O ! then his lines would ravish savage ears,
And plant in tyrants mild humility.

Act 4, Sc. 3.

SONG

When daisies pied and violets blue
And lady-smocks all silver-white
And cuckoo-buds of yellow hue
Do paint the meadows with delight,
The cuckoo then, on every tree,
Mocks married men; for thus sings he,
Cuckoo ;
Cuckoo, cuckoo : O, word of fear,
Unpleasing to a married ear!

When shepherds pipe on oaten straws,
And merry larks are ploughmen's clocks,
When turtles tread, and rooks, and daws,
And maidens bleach their summer smocks,
The cuckoo then, on every tree,
Mocks married men; for thus sings he,
Cuckoo ;
Cuckoo, cuckoo : O, word of fear,
Unpleasing to a married ear !

Act 5, Sc. 2.

WINTER

When icicles hang by the wall
  And Dick the shepherd blows his nail,
And Tom bears logs into the hall,
  And milk comes frozen home in pail;
When blood is nipt, and ways be foul,
Then nightly sings the staring owl
        Tu-whoo!
To-whit, Tu-whoo! A merry note!
While greasy Joan doth keel the pot.

When all about the wind both blow,
  And coughing drowns the parson's saw,
And birds sit brooding in the snow,
  And Marian's nose looks red and raw;
When roasted crabs hiss in the bowl—
Then nightly sings the staring owl
        Tu-whoo!
To-whit, Tu-whoo! A merry note!
While greasy Joan doth keel the pot.

Act 5, Sc. 2.

LOVE'S TRIALS

Ay me ! for aught that ever I could read,
Could ever hear by tale or history,
The course of truc love never did run smooth ;
But, either it was different in blood, . . .
Or else misgraffed in respect of years, . . .
Or else it stood upon the choice of friends, . . .
Or, if there were a sympathy in choice,
War, death, or sickness did lay siege to it,
Making it momentany as a sound,
Swift as a shadow, short as any dream,
Brief as the lightning in the collied night,
That, in a spleen, unfolds both heaven and
earth,
And ere a man hath power to say, ' Behold ! '
The jaws of darkness do devour it up :
So quick bright things come to confusion.

Act I, Sc. I.

LOVE'S BLINDNESS

Things base and vile, holding no quantity,
Love can transpose to form and dignity.
Love looks not with the eyes, but with the mind,
And therefore is wing'd Cupid painted blind.
Nor hath Love's mind of any judgment taste ;
Wings and no eyes figure unheedy haste :
And therefore is Love said to be a child,
Because in choice he is so oft beguil'd.
As waggish boys in game themselves forswear,
So the boy Love is perjur'd every where.

Act I, Sc. I.

LOVE-IN-IDLENESS

Thou remember'st
Since once I sat upon a promontory,
And heard a mermaid on a dolphin's back
Uttering such dulcet and harmonious breath,
That the rude sea grew civil at her song,
And certain stars shot madly from their spheres
To hear the sea-maid's music.
That very time I saw, but thou couldst not,
Flying between the cold moon and the earth,
Cupid all arm'd : a certain aim he took
At a fair vestal throned by the west,
And loos'd his love-shaft smartly from his bow.
As it should pierce a hundred thousand hearts ;
But I might see young Cupid's fiery shaft
Quench'd in the chaste beams of the wat'ry
moon,
And the imperial votaress passed on,
In maiden meditation, fancy-free.
Yet mark'd I where the bolt of Cupid fell :
It fell upon a little western flower,
Before milk-white, now purple with love's
wound,
And maidens call it, Love-in-idleness.

Act 2, Sc. 1.

PUCK'S SONG

Over hill, over dale,
  Thorough bush, thorough brier,
Over park, over pale,
  Thorough flood, thorough fire,
I do wander every where,
Swifter than the moone's sphere ;
And I serve the fairy queen,
To dew her orbs upon the green :
The cowslips tall her pensioners be ;
In their gold coats spots you see ;
Those be rubies, fairy favours,
In their freckles live their savours :
I must go seek some dew-drops here,
And hang a pearl in every cowslip's ear.

Act 2, Sc. 1.

FAIRY SONG

You spotted snakes with double tongue,
  Thorny hedge-hogs, be not seen ;
Newts and blind-worms, do no wrong ;
  Come not near our fairy queen :

  Philomel, with melody,
  Sing in our sweet lullaby ;
Lulla, lulla, lullaby, lulla, lulla, lullaby.
  Never harm, nor spell, nor charm,
  Come our lovely lady nigh ;
  So, good night, with lullaby.

Weaving spiders, come not here :
  Hence, you long-legged spinners, hence !
Beetles black, approach not near ;
  Worm, nor snail, do no offence.

  Philomel, with melody, &c,

Act 2, Sc. 2.

TITANIA'S BOWER

I know a bank whereon the wild thyme blows,
Where oxlips and the nodding violet grows
Quite over-canopied with luscious woodbine,
With sweet musk-roses, and with eglantine :
There sleeps Titania some time of the night,
Lull'd in these flowers with dances and delight ;
And there the snake throws her enamell'd skin,
Weed wide enough to wrap a fairy in :

Act 2, Sc. 2.

FAIRY SONG

Now the hungry lion roars,
  And the wolf behowls the moon ;
Whilst the heavy ploughman snores,
  All with weary task fordone.
Now the wasted brands do glow,
  Whilst the screech-owl, screeching loud,
Puts the wretch that lies in woe
  In remembrance of a shroud.
Now it is the time of night
  That the graves, all gaping wide,
Every one lets forth his sprite,
  In the churchway paths to glide :
And we fairies, that do run
  By the triple Hecate's team,
From the presence of the sun,
  Following darkness like a dream,
Now are frolic ; not a mouse
Shall disturb this hallowed house :
I am sent with broom before,
To sweep the dust behind the door.

Act 5, Sc. 1.

GRATIANO ON WISDOM

Let me play the fool:
With mirth and laughter let old wrinkles come,
And let my liver rather heat with wine
Than my heart cool with mortifying groans.
Why should a man, whose blood is warm within,
Sit like his grandsire cut in alabaster?
Sleep when he wakes, and creep into the jaundice
By being peevish? I tell thee what, Antonio—
I love thee, and it is my love that speaks—
There are a sort of men whose visages
Do cream and mantle like a standing pond,
And do a wilful stillness entertain,
With purpose to be dress'd in an opinion
Of wisdom, gravity, profound conceit;
As who should say, "I am Sir Oracle,
And when I ope my lips let no dog bark!"
O, my Antonio, I do know of these,
That therefore only are reputed wise
For saying nothing; when, I am very sure,
If they should speak, would almost damn those ears
Which, hearing them, would call their brothers fools.

Act I, Sc. I.

BASSANIO ON GRATIANO

Gratiano speaks an infinite deal of nothing, more than any man in all Venice. His reasons are as two grains of wheat hid in two bushels of chaff: you shall seek all day ere you find them, and, when you have them, they are not worth the search.

Act 1, Sc. 1.

PRECEPT AND PRACTICE

If to do were as easy as to know what were good to do, chapels had been churches, and poor men's cottages princes' palaces. It is a good divine that follows his own instructions: I can easier teach twenty what were good to be done, than be one of the twenty to follow mine own teaching. The brain may devise laws for the blood, but a hot temper leaps o'er a cold decree: such a hare is madness the youth, to skip o'er the meshes of good counsel the cripple.

Act 1, Sc. 2.

JOY OF SEEKING

O ! ten times faster Venus' pigeons fly
To seal love's bonds new-made, than they are wont
To keep obliged faith unforfeited !
Who riseth from a feast
With that keen appetite that he sits down ?
Where is the horse that doth untread again
His tedious measures with the unbated fire
That he did pace them first ? All things that are,
Are with more spirit chased than enjoy'd.
How like a younker or a prodigal
The scarfed bark puts from her native bay,
Hugg'd and embraced by the strumpet wind !
How like the prodigal doth she return,
With over-weather'd ribs and ragged sails,
Lean, rent, and beggar'd by the strumpet wind!

Act 2, Sc. 6.

THE TRUE SEED OF HONOUR

For who shall go about
To cozen fortune and be honourable
Without the stamp of merit? Let none presume
To wear an undeserved dignity.
O! that estates, degrees, and offices
Were not deriv'd corruptly, and that clear honour
Were purchas'd by the merit of the wearer.
How many then should cover that stand bare;
How many be commanded that command;
How much low peasantry would then be glean'd
From the true seed of honour; and how much honour
Pick'd from the chaff and ruin of the times
To be new varnish'd!

Act 2, Sc. 9.

SHYLOCK'S PROTESTATION

If it will feed nothing else, it will feed my revenge. He hath disgraced me, and hindered me half a million, laughed at my losses, mocked at my gains, scorned my nation, thwarted my bargains, cooled my friends, heated mine enemies; and what's his reason? I am a Jew. Hath not a Jew eyes? hath not a Jew hands, organs, dimensions, senses, affections, passions? fed with the same food, hurt with the same weapons, subject to the same diseases, healed by the same means, warmed and cooled by the same winter and summer, as a Christian is? If you prick us, do we not bleed? if you tickle us, do we not laugh? if you poison us, do we not die? and if you wrong us, shall we not revenge? If we are like you in the rest, we will resemble you in that. If a Jew wrong a Christian, what is his humility? Revenge. If a Christian wrong a Jew, what should his sufferance be by Christian example? Why, revenge. The villany you teach me I will execute, and it shall go hard but I will better the instruction.

Act 3, Sc. 1.

LET MUSIC SOUND

Let music sound while he doth make his choice ;
Then, if he lose, he makes a swan-like end,
Fading in music : that the comparison
May stand more proper, my eye shall be the
stream
And watery death-bed for him. He may win ;
And what is music then ? then music is
Even as the flourish when true subjects bow
To a new-crowned monarch : such it is
As are those dulcet sounds in break of day
That creep into the dreaming bridegroom's ear,
And summon him to marriage. Now he goes,
With no less presence, but with much more love,
Than young Alcides, when he did redeem
The virgin tribute paid by howling Troy
To the sea-monster : I stand for sacrifice ;
The rest aloof are the Dardanian wives,
With bleared visages, come forth to view
The issue of the exploit.

Act 3, Sc. 2.

FANCY

Tell me where is fancy bred,
Or in the heart, or in the head?
How begot, how nourishèd?
Reply, reply.

It is engendered in the eyes;
With gazing fed; and fancy dies
In the cradle where it lies.
Let us all ring fancy's knell;
I'll begin it:—Ding, dong, bell.
—Ding, dong, bell.

Act 3, Sc. 2.

MERCY

The quality of mercy is not strain'd,
It droppeth as the gentle rain from heaven
Upon the place beneath : it is twice bless'd ;
It blesseth him that gives and him that takes :
'Tis mightiest in the mightiest ; it becomes
The throned monarch better than his crown ;
His sceptre shows the force of temporal power,
The attribute to awe and majesty,
Wherein doth sit the dread and fear of kings ;
But mercy is above this sceptred sway,
It is enthroned in the hearts of kings,
It is an attribute to God himself,
And earthly power doth then show likest God's
When mercy seasons justice.

Act 4, Sc. 1.

THE MUSIC OF THE SPHERES

How sweet the moonlight sleeps upon this bank!
Here will we sit, and let the sounds of music
Creep in our ears : soft stillness and the night
Become the touches of sweet harmony.
Sit, Jessica : look, how the floor of heaven
Is thick inlaid with patines of bright gold :
There's not the smallest orb which thou be-
hold'st
But in his motion like an angel sings,
Still quiring to the young-eyed cherubins ;
Such harmony is in immortal souls.

Act 5, Sc. 1.

THE POWER OF MUSIC

I am never merry when I hear sweet music.
Lorenzo. The reason is, your spirits are attentive:
For do but note a wild and wanton herd,
Or race of youthful and unhandled colts,
Fetching mad bounds, bellowing and neighing loud.
Which is the hot condition of their blood ;
If they but hear perchance a trumpet sound,
Or any air of music touch their ears,
You shall perceive them make a mutual stand,
Their savage eyes turn'd to a modest gaze
By the sweet power of music : therefore the poet
Did feign that Orpheus drew trees, stones, and floods ;
Since nought so stockish, hard, and full of rage,
But music for the time doth change his nature.
The man that hath no music in himself,
Nor is not mov'd with concord of sweet sounds,
Is fit for treasons, stratagems, and spoils ;
The motions of his spirit are dull as night,
And his affections dark as Erebus :
Let no such man be trusted. Mark the music.

Act 5, Sc. 1.

NATURE'S WISDOM

Now, my co-mates and brothers in exile,
Hath not old custom made this life more sweet
Than that of painted pomp? Are not these woods
More free from peril than the envious court?
Here feel we but the penalty of Adam,
The seasons' difference; as, the icy fang
And churlish chiding of the winter's wind,
Which, when it bites and blows upon my body,
Even till I shrink with cold, I smile and say
"This is no flattery: these are counsellors
That feelingly persuade me what I am."
Sweet are the uses of adversity,
Which like the toad, ugly and venomous,
Wears yet a precious jewel in his head;
And this our life exempt from public haunt,
Finds tongues in trees, books in the running brooks,
Sermons in stones, and good in every thing.

Act 2, Sc. 1.

THE TRUE LOVER

O! thou didst then ne'er love so heartily.
If thou remember'st not the slightest folly
That ever love did make thee run into,
Thou hast not lov'd:
Or if thou hast not sat as I do now,
Wearing thy hearer with thy mistress' praise,
Thou hast not lov'd:
Or if thou hast not broke from company
Abruptly, as my passion now makes me,
Thou hast not lov'd.

Act 2, Sc. 4.

UNDER THE GREENWOOD TREE

Under the greenwood tree
Who loves to lie with me,
And tune his merry note
Unto the sweet bird's throat—
Come hither, come hither, come hither!
Here shall he see
No enemy
But winter and rough weather.

Who doth ambition shun
And loves to live i' the sun,
Seeking the food he eats
And pleased with what he gets—
Come hither, come hither, come hither!
Here shall he see
No enemy
But winter and rough weather.

Act 2, Sc. 5.

WINTER SONG

Blow, blow, thou winter wind,
Thou art not so unkind
As man's ingratitude ;
Thy tooth is not so keen
Because thou art not seen,
Although thy breath be rude.
Heigh ho ! sing heigh ho ! unto the green holly:
Most friendship is feigning, most loving mere
folly :
Then, heigh ho ! the holly !
This life is most jolly.

Freeze, freeze, thou bitter sky,
Thou dost not bite so nigh
As benefits forgot :
Though thou the waters warp,
Thy sting is not so sharp
As friend remembered not.
Heigh ho ! sing heigh ho ! unto the green holly:
Most friendship is feigning, most loving mere
folly :
Then, heigh ho ! the holly !
This life is most jolly.

Act 2, Sc. 7.

THE SEVEN AGES

All the world's a stage,
And all the men and women merely players :
They have their exits and their entrances ;
And one man in his time plays many parts,
His acts being seven ages. At first the infant,
Mewling and puking in the nurse's arms.
And then the whining school-boy, with his satchel,
And shining morning face, creeping like snail
Unwillingly to school. And then the lover,
Sighing like furnace, with a woful ballad
Made to his mistress' eyebrow. Then a soldier,
Full of strange oaths, and bearded like the pard,
Jealous in honour, sudden and quick in quarrel,
Seeking the bubble reputation
Even in the cannon's mouth. And then the justice,
In fair round belly with good capon lin'd,
With eyes severe, and beard of formal cut,
Full of wise saws and modern instances ;
And so he plays his part. The sixth age shifts
Into the lean and slipper'd pantaloon,
With spectacles on nose and pouch on side,
His youthful hose well sav'd, a world too wide
For his shrunk shank ; and his big manly voice,

Turning again toward childish treble, pipes
And whistles in his sound. Last scene of all
That ends this strange eventful history,
Is second childishness and mere oblivion,
Sans teeth, sans eyes, sans taste, sans everything.

Act 2, Sc. 7.

LOVE

Good shepherd, tell this youth what 'tis to love.
It is to be all made of sighs and tears :—
It is to be all made of faith and service :–
It is to be all made of fantasy,
All made of passion, and all made of wishes ;
All adoration, duty, and observance ;
All humbleness, all patience, and impatience ;
All purity, all trial, all obeisance ;
And so am I for Phebe.

Act 5, Sc. 2.

LOVERS LOVE THE SPRING

It was a lover and his lass,
  With a hey, and a ho, and hey nonino,
That o'er the green corn-field did pass
  In the spring-time, the only pretty ring-time,
When birds do sing, hey ding a ding, ding ;
  Sweet lovers love the spring.

Between the acres of the rye,
  With a hey, and a ho, and a hey nonino,
These pretty country folks would lie,
  In the spring-time, the only pretty ring-time,
When birds do sing, hey ding a ding, ding ;
  Sweet lovers love the spring.

This carol they began that hour,
  With a hey, and a ho, and a hey nonino,
How that a life was but a flower
  In the spring-time, the only pretty ring-time,
When birds do sing, hey ding a ding, ding ;
  Sweet lovers love the spring.

And therefore take the present time,
  With a hey, and a ho, and a hey nonino,

For love is crownèd with the prime
  In the spring-time, the only pretty ring-time,
When birds do sing, hey ding a ding, ding;
  Sweet lovers love the spring.

Act 5, Sc. 3.

WOMAN'S TONGUE

Think you a little din can daunt mine ears?
Have I not in my time heard lions roar?
Have I not heard the sea, puff'd up with winds,
Rage like an angry boar chafed with sweat?
Have I not heard great ordnance in the field,
And heaven's artillery thunder in the skies?
Have I not in a pitched battle heard
Loud 'larums, neighing steeds, and trumpets' clang?
And do you tell me of a woman's tongue,
That gives not half so great a blow to hear
As will a chestnut in a farmer's fire?

Act 1, Sc. 2.

THE MIND ENRICHES

Our purses shall be proud, our garments poor :
For 'tis the mind that makes the body rich ;
And as the sun breaks through the darkest
clouds,
So honour peereth in the meanest habit.
What, is the jay more precious than the lark
Because his feathers are more beautiful ?
Or is the adder better than the eel
Because his painted skin contents the eye ?
O, no, good Kate ! Neither art thou the worse
For this poor furniture and mean array.

Act 4, Sc. 3.

A WIFE'S DUTY

A woman mov'd is like a fountain troubled,
Muddy, ill-seeming, thick, bereft of beauty;
And while it is so, none so dry or thirsty
Will deign to sip or touch one drop of it.
Thy husband is thy lord, thy life, thy keeper,
Thy head, thy sovereign ; one that cares for
thee,
And for thy maintenance commits his body
To painful labour both by sea and land,
To watch the night in storms, the day in cold,
Whilst thou liest warm at home, secure and
safe ;
And craves no other tribute at thy hands
But love, fair looks, and true obedience ;
Too little payment for so great a debt.

Act 5, Sc. 2.

THE POWER WITHIN

Our remedies oft in ourselves do lie
Which we ascribe to heaven : the fated sky
Gives us free scope ; only doth backward pull
Our slow designs when we ourselves are dull.
What power is it which mounts my love so high;
That makes me see, and cannot feed mine eye ?
The mightiest space in fortune nature brings
To join like likes, and kiss like native things.
Impossible be strange attempts to those
That weigh their pains in sense, and do suppose
What hath been cannot be : who ever strove
To show her merit, that did miss her love ?

Act I, Sc. I.

ADVICE

Be thou blest, Bertram ; and succeed thy father
In manners, as in shape ! thy blood and virtue
Contend for empire in thee ; and thy goodness
Share with thy birthright ! Love all, trust a few,
Do wrong to none : be able for thine enemy
Rather in power than use, and keep thy friend
Under thy own life's key : be check'd for silence,
But never tax'd for speech.

Act I, Sc. I

HONOUR

From lowest place when virtuous things pro-
ceed,
The place is dignified by the doer's deed :
Where great additions swell 's, and virtue none,
It is a dropsied honour. Good alone
Is good without a name : vileness is so :
The property by what it is should go,
Not by the title. She is young, wise, fair ;
In these to nature she's immediate heir,
And these breed honour : that is honour's scorn
Which challenges itself as honour's born,
And is not like the sire : honours thrive
When rather from our acts we them derive
Than our foregoers. The mere word's a slave,
Debosh'd on every tomb, on every grave
A lying trophy, and as oft is dumb
Where dust and damn'd oblivion is the tomb
Of honour'd bones indeed.

Act 2, Sc. 3.

MUSIC

If music be the food of love, play on ;
Give me excess of it, that, surfeiting,
The appetite may sicken, and so die.
That strain again ! it had a dying fall :
O ! it came o'er my ear like the sweet sound
That breathes upon a bank of violets,
Stealing and giving odour. Enough ! no more:
'Tis not so sweet now as it was before.
O spirit of love ! how quick and fresh art thou,
That, notwithstanding thy capacity
Receiveth as the sea, nought enters there,
Of what validity and pitch soe'er,
But falls into abatement and low price,
Even in a minute : so full of shapes is fancy,
That it alone is high fantastical.

Act I, Sc. I.

VIOLA'S PLEA

Make me a willow cabin at your gate,
And call upon my soul within the house;
Write loyal cantons of contemned love,
And sing them loud even in the dead of night;
Holla your name to the reverberate hills,
And make the babbling gossip of the air
Cry out, "Olivia!" O! you should not rest
Between the elements of air and earth,
But you should pity me!

Act 1, Sc. 5.

TRUE LOVE

Come hither, boy: if ever thou shalt love,
In the sweet pangs of it remember me;
For such as I am all true lovers are:
Unstaid and skittish in all motions else
Save in the constant image of the creature
That is belov'd.

Act 2, Sc. 4.

O MISTRESS MINE

O Mistress mine, where are you roaming?
O stay and hear! your true-love's coming
That can sing both high and low;
Trip no further, pretty sweeting,
Journeys end in lovers' meeting—
Every wise man's son doth know.

What is love? 'tis not hereafter;
Present mirth hath present laughter;
What's to come is still unsure:
In delay there lies no plenty,—
Then come kiss me, Sweet-and-twenty,
Youth's a stuff will not endure.

Act 2, Sc. 3.

COME AWAY, DEATH

Come away, come away, Death,
And in sad cypres let me be laid ;
Fly away, fly away, breath ;
I am slain by a fair cruel maid.
My shroud of white, stuck all with yew,
O prepare it !
My part of death no one so true
Did share it.

Not a flower, not a flower sweet
On my black coffin let there be strown ;
Not a friend, not a friend greet
My poor corpse, where my bones shall be
thrown ;
A thousand thousand sighs to save,
Lay me, O where
Sad true lover never find my grave,
To weep there.

Act 2, Sc. 4.

A GARLAND FOR YOUTH

O Proserpina !
For the flowers now that frighted thou let'st fall
From Dis's waggon! daffodils,
That come before the swallow dares, and take
The winds of March with beauty; violets dim,
But sweeter than the lids of Juno's eyes
Or Cytherea's breath ; pale prime-roses,
That die unmarried, ere they can behold
Bright Phœbus in his strength, a malady
Most incident to maids ; bold oxlips and
The crown imperial ; lilies of all kinds,
The flower-de-luce being one. O ! these I lack
To make you garlands of, and my sweet friend,
To strew him o'er and o'er !

Act 4, Sc. 3.

• • • • •

Jog on, jog on, the footpath way
And merrily hent the stile-a :
A merry heart goes all the day,
Your sad tires in a mile-a.

Act 4, Sc. 2.

A LOVER'S COMMENDATION

What you do
Still betters what is done. When you speak, sweet,
I'd have you do it ever : when you sing,
I'd have you buy and sell so ; so give alms ;
Pray so : and, for the ordering your affairs,
To sing them too : when you do dance, I wish you
A wave o' the sea, that you might ever do
Nothing but that ; move still, still so,
And own no other function : each your doing,
So singular in each particular,
Crowns what you are doing in the present deed,
That all your acts are queens.

Act 4, Sc. 3.

TO PAINT THE LILY

To guard a title that was rich before,
To gild refined gold, to paint the lily,
To throw a perfume on the violet,
To smooth the ice, or add another hue
Unto the rainbow, or with taper-light
To seek the beauteous eye of heaven to garnish,
Is wasteful and ridiculous excess.

Act 4, Sc. 2.

ENGLAND INVINCIBLE

This England never did, nor never shall,
Lie at the proud foot of a conqueror,
But when it first did help to wound itself.
Now these her princes are come home again,
Come the three corners of the world in arms,
And we shall shock them. Nought shall make
us rue,
If England to itself do rest but true.

Act 5, Sc. 7.

IN PRAISE OF ENGLAND

This royal throne of kings, this scepter'd isle,
This earth of majesty, this seat of Mars,
This other Eden, demi-paradise,
This fortress built by Nature for herself
Against infection and the hand of war,
This happy breed of men, this little world,
This precious stone set in the silver sea,
Which serves it in the office of a wall,
Or as a moat defensive to a house,
Against the envy of less happier lands,
This blessed plot, this earth, this realm, this
England,

England, bound in with the triumphant sea,
Whose rocky shore beats back the envious siege
Of watery Neptune, is now bound in with
shame,
With inky blots, and rotten parchment bonds :
That England, that was wont to conquer others,
Hath made a shameful conquest of itself.

Act 2, Sc. 1.

CONSOLATION IN EXILE

Gaunt. All places that the eye of heaven visits
Are to a wise man ports and happy havens.
Teach thy necessity to reason thus ;
There is no virtue like necessity.
Think not the king did banish thee,
But thou the king. Woe doth the heavier sit,
Where it perceives it is but faintly borne.
Go, say I sent thee forth to purchase honour,
And not the king exil'd thee ; or suppose
Devouring pestilence hangs in our air,
And thou art flying to a fresher clime.
Look, what thy soul holds dear, imagine it
To lie that way thou go'st, not whence thou com'st.
Suppose the singing birds musicians,
The grass whereon thou tread'st the presence strew'd,
The flowers fair ladies, and thy steps no more
Than a delightful measure or a dance ;
For gnarling sorrow hath less power to bite
The man that mocks at it and sets it light.
Bolingbroke. O ! who can hold a fire in his hand
By thinking on the frosty Caucasus ?
Or cloy the hungry edge of appetite

By bare imagination of a feast?
Or wallow naked in December snow
By thinking on fantastic summer's heat?
O, no! the apprehension of the good
Gives but the greater feeling to the worse:
Fell sorrow's tooth doth never rankle more
Than when it bites, but lanceth not the sore.

Act 1, Sc. 3.

REPUTATION

My dear dear lord,
The purest treasure mortal times afford
Is spotless reputation: that away,
Men are but gilded loam or painted clay.
A jewel in a ten-times-barr'd-up chest
Is a bold spirit in a loyal breast.
Mine honour is my life; both grow in one;
Take honour from me, and my life is done:

Act 1, Sc. 1.

RUMOUR

Open your ears ; for which of you will stop
The vent of hearing when loud Rumour speaks?
I, from the orient to the drooping west,
Making the wind my post-horse, still unfold
The acts commenced on this ball of earth :
Upon my tongues continual slanders ride,
The which in every language I pronounce,
Stuffing the ears of men with false reports.
I speak of peace, while covert enmity
Under the smile of safety wounds the world :
And who but Rumour, who but only I,
Make fearful musters and prepar'd defence,
Whilst the big year, swoln with some other grief,
Is thought with child by the stern tyrant war,
And no such matter? Rumour is a pipe
Blown by surmises, jealousies, conjectures,
And of so easy and so plain a stop
That the blunt monster with uncounted heads,
The still-discordant wavering multitude,
Can play upon it.

Induction.

HENRY IV'S SON

For he is gracious, if he be observ'd :
He hath a tear for pity and a hand
Open as day for melting charity ;
Yet, notwithstanding, being incens'd, he's flint ;
As humorous as winter, and as sudden
As flaws congealed in the spring of day.
His temper therefore must be well observ'd :
Chide him for faults, and do it reverently,
When you perceive his blood inclin'd to mirth ;
But, being moody, give him line and scope,
Till that his passions, like a whale on ground,
Confound themselves with working.

Act 4, Sc. 4.

ON FORTUNE

Will Fortune never come with both hands full
But write her fair words still in foulest letters ?
She either gives a stomach and no food ;
Such are the poor, in health ; or else a feast
And takes away the stomach ; such are the rich,
That have abundance and enjoy it not.

Act 4, Sc. 4.

AN ORDERED COMMONWEALTH

Therefore doth heaven divide
The state of man in divers functions,
Setting endeavour in continual motion ;
To which is fixed, as an aim or butt,
Obedience : for so work the honey-bees,
Creatures that by a rule in nature teach
The act of order to a peopled kingdom.
They have a king and officers of sorts ;
Where some, like magistrates, correct at home,
Others, like merchants, venture trade abroad,
Others, like soldiers, armed in their stings,
Make boot upon the summer's velvet buds ;
Which pillage they with merry march bring
home
To the tent-royal of their emperor :
Who, busied in his majesty, surveys
The singing masons building roofs of gold,
The civil citizens kneading up the honey,
The poor mechanic porters crowding in
Their heavy burdens at his narrow gate,
The sad-ey'd justice, with his surly hum,
Delivering o'er to executors pale
The lazy yawning drone.

Act 1, Sc. 2.

HENRY V. BEFORE HARFLEUR

Once more unto the breach, dear friends, once more ;
Or close the wall up with our English dead !
In peace there's nothing so becomes a man
As modest stillness and humility :
But when the blast of war blows in our ears,
Then imitate the action of the tiger ;
Stiffen the sinews, summon up the blood,
Disguise fair nature with hard-favour'd rage ;
Then lend the eye a terrible aspect ;
Let it pry through the portage of the head
Like the brass cannon; let the brow o'erwhelm it
As fearfully as doth a galled rock
O'erhang and jutty his confounded base,
Swill'd with the wild and wasteful ocean.
Now set the teeth and stretch the nostril wide,
Hold hard the breath, and bend up every spirit
To his full height ! On, on, you noblest English !
Whose blood is fet from fathers of war-proof;
Fathers that, like so many Alexanders,
Have in these parts from morn till even fought,
And sheath'd their swords for lack of argument.
Dishonour not your mothers ; now attest

That those whom you call'd fathers did beget
you.
Be copy now to men of grosser blood,
And teach them how to war. And you, good
yeomen,
Whose limbs were made in England, show us
here
The mettle of your pasture ; let us swear
That you are worth your breeding ; which I
doubt not ;
For there is none of you so mean and base
That hath not noble lustre in your eyes.
I see you stand like greyhounds in the slips,
Straining upon the start. The game's afoot :
Follow your spirit ; and, upon this charge
Cry " God for Harry ! England and Saint
George ! "

Act 3. Sc. 1.

HENRY V. BEFORE AGINCOURT

This day is call'd the feast of Crispian :
He that outlives this day, and comes safe home,
Will stand a tip-toe when this day is nam'd,
And rouse him at the name of Crispian.
He that shall live this day, and see old age,
Will yearly on the vigil feast his neighbours,

And say, " To-morrow is Saint Crispian : "
Then will he strip his sleeve and show his scars,
And say, " These wounds I had on Crispin's day."
Old men forget : yet all shall be forgot,
But he'll remember with advantages
What feats he did that day. Then shall our names,
Familiar in his mouth as household words,
Harry the king, Bedford and Exeter,
Warwick and Talbot, Salisbury and Gloucester,
Be in their flowing cups freshly remember'd.
This story shall the good man teach his son ;
And Crispin Crispian shall ne'er go by,
From this day to the ending of the world,
But we in it shall be remembered ;
We few, we happy few, we band of brothers ;
For he to-day that sheds his blood with me
Shall be my brother ; be he ne'er so vile
This day shall gentle his condition :
And gentlemen in England now a-bed
Shall think themselves accurs'd they were not here,
And hold their manhoods cheap whiles any speaks
That fought with us upon Saint Crispin's day.

Act 4, Sc. 3.

THE SIMPLE LIFE

O God ! methinks it were a happy life,
To be no better than a homely swain ;
To sit upon a hill, as I do now,
To carve out dials quaintly, point by point,
Thereby to see the minutes how thy run,
How many make the hour full complete ;
How many hours bring about the day ;
How many days will finish up the year ;
How many years a mortal man may live.
When this is known, then to divide the times :
So many hours must I tend my flock ;
So many hours must I take my rest ;
So many hours must I contemplate ;
So many hours must I sport myself ;
So many days my ewes have been with young ;
So many weeks ere the poor fools will ean ;
So many years ere I shall shear the fleece :
So minutes, hours, days, months, and years,
Pass'd over to the end they were created,
Would bring white hairs unto a quiet grave.
Ah ! what a life were this ! how sweet ! how
lovely !
Gives not the hawthorn bush a sweeter shade
To shepherds, looking on their silly sheep,
Than doth a rich embroider'd canopy

To kings, that fear their subjects' treachery?
O, yes! it doth; a thousand-fold it doth.
And to conclude, the shepherd's homely curds,
His cold thin drink out of his leather bottle,
His wonted sleep under a fresh tree's shade,
All which secure and sweetly he enjoys,
Is far beyond a prince's delicates,
His viands sparkling in a golden cup,
His body couched in a curious bed,
When care, mistrust, and treason wait on him.

Act 2, Sc. 5.

INTEGRITY

What stronger breastplate than a heart untainted!
Thrice is he arm'd that hath his quarrel just,
And he but naked, though lock'd up in steel,
Whose conscience with injustice is corrupted.

(King Henry the Sixth, Part 2.) Act 3, Sc. 2.

A PRAYER FOR PEACE

And let their heirs—God, if thy will be so,—
Enrich the time to come with smooth-fac'd
peace,
With smiling plenty, and fair prosperous days !
Abate the edge of traitors, gracious Lord,
That would reduce these bloody days again,
And make poor England weep in streams of
blood !
Let them not live to taste this land's increase,
That would with treason wound this fair land's
peace !
Now civil wounds are stopp'd, peace lives again:
That she may long live here, God say amen !

Act 5, Sc. 5.

MUSIC

Orpheus with his lute made trees,
And the mountain-tops that freeze,
  Bow themselves when he did sing :
To his music plants and flowers
Ever sprung ; as sun and showers
  There had made a lasting spring.

Everything that heard him play,
Ev'n the billows of the sea,
  Hung their heads, and then lay by.
In sweet music is such art :
Killing care and grief of heart
Fall asleep, or, hearing, die.

Act 3, Sc. 1.

WOLSEY ADDRESSES CROMWELL

Cromwell, I charge thee, fling away ambition :
By that sin fell the angels ; how can man then,
The image of his Maker, hope to win by't ?
Love thyself last : cherish those hearts that hate
thee ;
Corruption wins not more than honesty.
Still in thy right hand carry gentle peace,
To silence envious tongues : be just, and fear
not.
Let all the ends thou aim'st at be thy country's,
Thy God's, and truth's ; then if thou fall'st, O
Cromwell !
Thou fall'st a blessed martyr. Serve the king ;
And,—prithee, lead me in :
There take an inventory of all I have,
To the last penny ; 'tis the king's : my robe,
And my integrity to heaven is all
I dare now call mine own. O Cromwell, Crom-
well !
Had I but serv'd my God with half the zeal
I serv'd my king, he would not in mine age
Have left me naked to mine enemies.

Act 3, Sc. 2.

WOLSEY'S SPEECH

So farewell to the little good you bear me.
Farewell ! a long farewell, to all my greatness !
This is the state of man : to-day he puts forth
The tender leaves of hopes ; to-morrow blossoms,
And bears his blushing honours thick upon him;
The third day comes a frost, a killing frost ;
And, when he thinks, good easy man, full surely
His greatness is a-ripening, nips his root,
And then he falls, as I do. I have ventur'd,
Like little wanton boys that swim on bladders,
This many summers in a sea of glory,
But far beyond my depth : my high-blown pride
At length broke under me, and now has left me,
Weary and old with service, to the mercy
Of a rude stream, that must for ever hide me.
Vain pomp and glory of this world, I hate ye :
I feel my heart new open'd. O ! how wretched
Is that poor man that hangs on princes' favours!
There is, betwixt that smile we would aspire to,
That sweet aspect of princes, and their ruin,
More pangs and fears than wars or women have ;
And when he falls, he falls like Lucifer,
Never to hope again.

Act 3, Sc. 2.

ACTIVE HONOUR

Time hath, my lord, a wallet at his back,
Wherein he puts alms for oblivion,
A great-siz'd monster of ingratitudes :
Those scraps are good deeds past ; which are devour'd
As fast as they are made, forgot as soon
As done : perseverance, dear my lord,
Keeps honour bright : to have done, is to hang
Quite out of fashion, like a rusty mail
In monumental mockery. Take the instant way;
For honour travels in a strait so narrow
Where one but goes abreast : keep, then, the path ;
For emulation hath a thousand sons
That one by one pursue : if you give way,
Or hedge aside from the direct forthright,
Like to an enter'd tide they all rush by
And leave you hindmost ;
Or, like a gallant horse fall'n in first rank,
Lie there for pavement to the abject rear,
O'errun and trampled on : then what they do in present,
Though less than yours in past, must o'ertop yours ;

For time is like a fashionable host,
That slightly shakes his parting guest by the hand,
And with his arms outstretch'd, as he would fly,
Grasps in the comer : welcome ever smiles,
And farewell goes out sighing. O ! let not virtue seek
Remuneration for the thing it was ;
For beauty, wit,
High birth, vigour of bone, desert in service,
Love, friendship, charity, are subjects all
To envious and calumniating time.
One touch of nature makes the whole world kin,
That all with one consent praise new-born gawds,
Though they are made and moulded of things past,
And give to dust that is a little gilt
More laud than gilt o'er-dusted.
The present eye praises the present object.

Act 3, Sc. 3.

ENVY TRANSMUTED TO LOVE

O Marcius, Marcius !
Each word thou hast spoke hath weeded from my heart
A root of ancient envy. If Jupiter
Should from yond cloud speak divine things,
And say, " 'Tis true," I'd not believe them more
Than thee, all noble Marcius. Let me twine
Mine arms about that body, where against
My grained ash a hundred times hath broke,
And scarr'd the moon with splinters : here I clip
The anvil of my sword, and do contest
As hotly and as nobly with thy love
As ever in ambitious strength I did
Contend against thy valour. Know thou first,
I lov'd the maid I married ; never man
Sigh'd truer breath ; but that I see thee here,
Thou noble thing ! more dances my rapt heart
Than when I first my wedded mistress saw
Bestride my threshold. Why, thou Mars ! I tell thee,
We have a power on foot ; and I had purpose
Once more to hew thy target from thy brawn,
Or lose mine arm for't. Thou hast beat me out
Twelve several times, and I have nightly since

Dreamt of encounters 'twixt thyself and me ;
We have been down together in my sleep,
Unbuckling helms, fisting each other's throat,
And wak'd half dead with nothing.

Act 4, Sc. 5.

WHAT IS LOVE?

Love is a smoke rais'd with the fume of sighs ;
Being purg'd, a fire sparkling in lovers' eyes ;
Being vex'd, a sea nourish'd with lovers' tears :
What is it else? a madness most discreet,
A choking gall, and a preserving sweet.

Act 1, Sc. 1.

JULIET'S BEAUTY

O ! she doth teach the torches to burn bright.
It seems she hangs upon the cheek of night
Like a rich jewel in an Ethiop's ear ;
Beauty too rich for use, for earth too dear !
So shows a snowy dove trooping with crows,
As yonder lady o'er her fellows shows.
The measure done, I'll watch her place of stand,
And, touching hers, make blessed my rude hand.
Did my heart love till now ? forswear it, sight !
For I ne'er saw true beauty till this night.

Act 1, Sc. 5.

WHAT'S IN A NAME?

What's in a name? that which we call a rose
By any other name would smell as sweet;
So Romeo would, were he not Romeo call'd,
Retain that dear perfection which he owes
Without that title. Romeo, doff thy name;
And for that name, which is no part of thee,
Take all myself.

Act 2, Sc. 2.

ROMEO SPEAKS

But, soft! what light through yonder window
breaks?
It is the east, and Juliet is the sun!
Arise, fair sun, and kill the envious moon,
Who is already sick and pale with grief,
That thou her maid art far more fair than she:
Be not her maid, since she is envious;
Her vestal livery is but sick and green,
And none but fools do wear it; cast it off.
It is my lady; O! it is my love:
O! that she knew she were.
She speaks, yet she says nothing: what of that?

Her eye discourses ; I will answer it.
I am too bold, 'tis not to me she speaks :
Two of the fairest stars in all the heaven,
Having some business, do entreat her eyes
To twinkle in their spheres till they return.
What if her eyes were there, they in her head ?
The brightness of her cheek would shame those
stars
As daylight doth a lamp ; her eyes in heaven
Would through the airy region stream so bright
That birds would sing and think it were not
night.
See ! how she leans her cheek upon her hand :
O ! that I were a glove upon that hand,
That I might touch that cheek.

Act 2, Sc. 2

LOVE'S MESSENGERS

Love's heralds should be thoughts,
Which ten times faster glide than the sun's beams,
Driving back shadows over lowering hills :
Therefore do nimble-pinion'd doves draw Love,
And therefore hath the wind-swift Cupid wings.

Act 2, Sc. 5.

JULIET

How oft when men are at the point of death
Have they been merry! which their keepers call
A lightning before death : O! how may I
Call this a lightning? O my love! my wife!
Death, that hath suck'd the honey of thy breath,
Hath had no power yet upon thy beauty :
Thou art not conquer'd ; beauty's ensign yet
Is crimson in thy lips and in thy cheeks,
And death's pale flag is not advanced there.

Act 5, Sc. 3.

FRIENDSHIP

O you gods! think I, what need we have any friends, if we should ne'er have need of 'em? they were the most needless creatures living should we ne'er have use for 'em, and would most resemble sweet instruments hung up in cases, that keep their sounds to themselves. Why, I have often wished myself poorer that I might come nearer to you. We are born to do benefits: and what better or properer can we call our own than the riches of our friends? O! what a precious comfort 'tis, to have so many, like brothers, commanding one another's fortunes.

Act 1, Sc. 2.

PROMISE AND PERFORMANCE

Promising is the very air o' the time; it opens the eyes of expectation; performance is ever the duller for his act; and, but in the plainer and simpler kind of people, the deed of saying is quite out of use. To promise is most courtly and fashionable; performance is a kind of will or testament which argues a great sickness in his judgment that makes it.

Act 5, Sc. 1.

CASSIUS ON CÆSAR

Why, man, he doth bestride the narrow world
Like a Colossus ; and we petty men
Walk under his huge legs, and peep about
To find ourselves dishonourable graves.
Men at some time are masters of their fates :
The fault, dear Brutus, is not in our stars,
But in ourselves, that we are underlings.
Brutus and Cæsar : what should be in that
"Cæsar ? "
Why should that name be sounded more than
yours ?
Write them together, yours is as fair a name ;
Sound them, it doth become the mouth as
well ;
Weigh them, it is as heavy ; conjure with 'em,
" Brutus " will start a spirit as soon as " Cæsar."

Act 1, Sc. 2.

STRENGTH OF SPIRIT

I know where I will wear this dagger then ;
Cassius from bondage will deliver Cassius :
Therein, ye gods, you make the weak most
strong ;
Therein, ye gods, you tyrants do defeat :
Nor stony tower, nor walls of beaten brass,
Nor airless dungeon, nor strong links of iron,
Can be retentive to the strength of spirit ;
But life, being weary of those worldly bars,
Never lacks power to dismiss itself.
If I know this, know all the world besides,
That part of tyranny that I do bear
I can shake off at pleasure.

Act 1, Sc. 3.

DEATH INEVITABLE

Cæsar. What can be avoided
Whose end is purpos'd by the mighty gods?
Yet Cæsar shall go forth; for these predictions
Are to the world in general as to Cæsar.
Calphurnia. When beggars die there are no comets seen;
The heavens themselves blaze forth the death of princes.
Cæsar. Cowards die many times before their deaths;
The valiant never taste of death but once.
Of all the wonders that I yet have heard,
It seems to me most strange that men should fear;
Seeing that death, a necessary end,
Will come when it will come.

Act 2, Sc. 2.

ANTONY'S SORROW

O mighty Cæsar! dost thou lie so low?
Are all thy conquests, glories, triumphs, spoils,
Shrunk to this little measure? Fare thee well.
I know not, gentlemen, what you intend,
Who else must be let blood, who else is rank:
If I myself, there is no hour so fit
As Cæsar's death's hour, nor no instrument
Of half that worth as those your swords, made rich
With the most noble blood of all this world.
I do beseech ye, if ye bear me hard,
Now, whilst your purpled hands do reek and smoke,
Fulfil your pleasure. Live a thousand years,
I shall not find myself so apt to die:
No place will please me so, no mean of death,
As here by Cæsar, and by you cut off,
The choice and master spirits of this age.

Act 3, Sc. 1.

BRUTUS' JUSTIFICATION

If there be any in this assembly, any dear friend of Cæsar's, to him I say, that Brutus' love to Cæsar was no less than his. If then that friend demand why Brutus rose against Cæsar, this is my answer : Not that I loved Cæsar less, but that I loved Rome more. Had you rather Cæsar were living, and die all slaves, than that Cæsar were dead, to live all free men ? As Cæsar loved me, I weep for him ; as he was fortunate, I rejoice at it ; as he was valiant, I honour him ; but, as he was ambitious, I slew him. There is tears for his love ; joy for his fortune ; honour for his valour ; and death for his ambition. Who is here so base that would be a bondman ? If any, speak ; for him have I offended. Who is here so rude that would not be a Roman ? If any, speak ; for him have I offended. Who is here so vile that will not love his country ? If any, speak ; for him have I offended.

Act 3, Sc. 2.

ANTONY'S ORATION

Friends, Romans, countrymen, lend me your
ears ;
I come to bury Cæsar, not to praise him.
The evil that men do lives after them,
The good is oft interred with their bones ;
So let it be with Cæsar. The noble Brutus
Hath told you Cæsar was ambitious ;
If it were so, it was a grievous fault,
And grievously hath Cæsar answer'd it.
Here, under leave of Brutus and the rest,—
For Brutus is an honourable man ;
So are they all, all honourable men,—
Come I to speak in Cæsar's funeral.
He was my friend, faithful and just to me :
But Brutus says he was ambitious ;
And Brutus is an honourable man.
He hath brought many captives home to Rome,
Whose ransoms did the general coffers fill :
Did this in Cæsar seem ambitious ?
When that the poor have cried, Cæsar hath
wept ;
Ambition should be made of sterner stuff :
Yet Brutus says he was ambitious ;
And Brutus is an honourable man.
You all did see that on the Lupercal

I thrice presented him a kingly crown,
Which he did thrice refuse : was this ambition ?
Yet Brutus says he was ambitious ;
And, sure, he is an honourable man.
I speak not to disprove what Brutus spoke,
But here I am to speak what I do know.
You all did love him once, not without cause :
What cause withholds you then to mourn for
him ?
O judgment ! thou art fled to brutish beasts,
And men have lost their reason. Bear with me ;
My heart is in the coffin there with Cæsar,
And I must pause till it come back to me.

Act 3, Sc. 2.

ANTONY ON BRUTUS

This was the noblest Roman of them all ;
All the conspirators save only he
Did that they did in envy of great Cæsar ;
He only, in a general honest thought
And common good to all, made one of them.
His life was gentle, and the elements
So mix'd in him that Nature might stand up
And say to all the world, " This was a man ! "

Act 5, Sc. 5.

OPPORTUNITY

You must note beside,
That we have tried the utmost of our friends,
Our legions are brim-full, our cause is ripe :
The enemy increaseth every day ;
We, at the height, are ready to decline.
There is a tide in the affairs of men,
Which, taken at the flood, leads on to fortune ;
Omitted, all the voyage of their life
Is bound in shallows and in miseries.
On such a full sea are we now afloat ;
And we must take the current when it serves,
Or lose our ventures.

Act 4, Sc. 3.

MACBETH'S IRRESOLUTION

If it were done when 'tis done, then 'twere well
It were done quickly; if the assassination
Could trammel up the consequence, and catch
With his surcease success; that but this blow
Might be the be-all and the end-all here,
But here, upon this bank and shoal of time,
We'd jump the life to come. But in these cases
We still have judgment here; that we but teach
Bloody instructions, which, being taught, return
To plague the inventor; this even-handed justice
Commends the ingredients of our poison'd chalice
To our own lips. He's here in double trust:
First, as I am his kinsman and his subject,
Strong both against the deed; then, as his host,
Who should against his murderer shut the door,
Not bear the knife myself. Besides, this Duncan
Hath borne his faculties so meek, hath been
So clear in his great office, that his virtues
Will plead like angels trumpet-tongu'd against
The deep damnation of his taking-off;
And pity, like a naked new-born babe,
Striding the blast, or heaven's cherubin, hors'd

Upon the sightless couriers of the air,
Shall blow the horrid deed in every eye,
That tears shall drown the wind. I have no spur
To prick the sides of my intent, but only
Vaulting ambition, which o'er-leaps itself
And falls on the other.

Act 1, Sc. 7.

IS THIS A DAGGER?

Is this a dagger which I see before me,
The handle toward my hand? Come, let me
clutch thee:
I have thee not, and yet I see thee still.
Art thou not, fatal vision, sensible
To feeling as to sight? or art thou but
A dagger of the mind, a false creation,
Proceeding from the heat-oppressed brain?
I see thee yet, in form as palpable
As this which now I draw.
Thou marshall'st me the way that I was going;
And such an instrument I was to use.
Mine eyes are made the fools o' the other senses,
Or else worth all the rest: I see thee still;
And on thy blade and dudgeon gouts of blood,

Which was not so before. There's no such
thing :
It is the bloody business which informs
Thus to mine eyes. Now o'er the one half-
world
Nature seems dead, and wicked dreams abuse
The curtain'd sleep ; witchcraft celebrates
Pale Hecate's offerings ; and wither'd murder,
Alarum'd by his sentinel, the wolf,
Whose howl's his watch, thus with his stealthy
pace,
With Tarquin's ravishing strides, toward his
design
Moves like a ghost. Thou sure and firm-set
earth,
Hear not my steps, which way they walk, for fear
The very stones prate of my whereabout,
And take the present horror from the time,
Which now suits with it.

Act 2, Sc. 1.

THE SLEEP-WALKING SCENE

Enter Lady Macbeth, *with a taper.*

This is her very guise ; and, upon my life, fast asleep. Observe her ; stand close.

Doctor. How came she by that light ?

Gentlewoman. Why, it stood by her : she has light by her continually ; 'tis her command.

Doctor. You see, her eyes are open.

Gentlewoman. Ay, but their sense is shut.

Doctor. What is it she does now ? Look, how she rubs her hands.

Gentlewoman. It is an accustomed action with her, to seem thus washing her hands : I have known her continue in this a quarter of an hour.

Lady Macbeth. Yet here's a spot.

Doctor. Hark ! she speaks : I will set down what comes from her, to satisfy my remembrance the more strongly.

Lady Macbeth. Out, damned spot ! out, I say !—One ; two : why, then 'tis time to do't: —Hell is murky !—Fie, my lord, fie ! a soldier, and afeard ? What need we fear who knows it, when none can call our power to account ?— Yet who would have thought the old man to have had so much blood in him ? . . . .

The Thane of Fife had a wife; where is she now?—What, will these hands ne'er be clean?—No more o' that, my lord, no more o' that: you mar all with this starting.

Here's the smell of the blood still: all the perfumes of Arabia will not sweeten this little hand. Oh, oh, oh!

Wash your hands, put on your nightgown; look not so pale:—I tell you yet again, Banquo's buried; he cannot come out on's grave.

To bed, to bed; there's knocking at the gate: come, come, come, come, give me your hand: what's done cannot be undone: to bed, to bed, to bed.

Act 5, Sc. 1.

A MIND DISEAS'D

Canst thou not minister to a mind diseas'd;
Pluck from the memory a rooted sorrow;
Raze out the written troubles of the brain;
And with some sweet oblivious antidote
Cleanse the stuff'd bosom of that perilous stuff
Which weighs upon the heart?

Act 5, Sc. 3.

OLD AGE

I have liv'd long enough : my way of life
Is fall'n into the sear, the yellow leaf ;
And that which should accompany old age,
As honour, love, obedience, troops of friends,
I must not look to have ; but, in their stead,
Curses, not loud but deep, mouth-honour, breath,
Which the poor heart would fain deny, and dare not.

Act 5, Sc. 3.

REFLECTIONS ON LIFE

To-morrow, and to-morrow, and to-morrow,
Creeps in this petty pace from day to day,
To the last syllable of recorded time ;
And all our yesterdays have lighted fools
The way to dusty death. Out, out, brief candle !
Life's but a walking shadow, a poor player
That struts and frets his hour upon the stage,
And then is heard no more ; it is a tale
Told by an idiot, full of sound and fury,
Signifying nothing.

Act 5, Sc. 4.

THE BIRD OF DAWNING

It faded on the crowing of the cock.
Some say that ever 'gainst that season comes
Wherein our Saviour's birth is celebrated,
The bird of dawning singeth all night long ;
And then, they say, no spirit can walk abroad ;
The nights are wholesome ; then no planets
strike,
No fairy takes, nor witch hath power to charm,
So hallow'd and so gracious is the time.

Act 1, Sc. 1.

ON HIS MOTHER'S MARRIAGE

O ! that this too too solid flesh would melt,
Thaw and resolve itself into a dew ;
Or that the Everlasting had not fix'd
His canon 'gainst self-slaughter ! O God ! O
God !
How weary, stale, flat, and unprofitable
Seem to me all the uses of this world.
Fie on't ! O fie ! 'tis an unweeded garden,
That grows to seed ; things rank and gross in
nature

Possess it merely. That it should come to this !
But two months dead : nay, not so much, not
two :
So excellent a king ; that was, to this,
Hyperion to a satyr ; so loving to my mother
That he might not beteem the winds of heaven
Visit her face too roughly. Heaven and earth !
Must I remember ? why, she would hang on
him,
As if increase of appetite had grown
By what it fed on ; and yet, within a month,
Let me not think on't : Frailty, thy name is
woman !
A little month ; or ere those shoes were old
With which she follow'd my poor father's body,
Like Niobe, all tears ; why she, even she,—
O God ! a beast, that wants discourse of reason,
Would have mourn'd longer,—married with
mine uncle,
My father's brother, but no more like my father
Than I to Hercules : within a month,
Ere yet the salt of most unrighteous tears
Had left the flushing in her galled eyes,
She married.

Act 1, Sc. 2.

ADVICE TO A SON

Give thy thoughts no tongue,
Nor any unproportion'd thought his act.
Be thou familiar, but by no means vulgar ;
The friends thou hast, and their adoption tried,
Grapple them to thy soul with hoops of steel ;
But do not dull thy palm with entertainment
Of each new-hatch'd, unfledg'd comrade. Beware
Of entrance to a quarrel, but, being in,
Bear't that th' opposed may beware of thee.
Give every man thine ear, but few thy voice ;
Take each man's censure, but reserve thy judgment.
Costly thy habit as thy purse can buy,
But not express'd in fancy ; rich, not gaudy ;
For the apparel oft proclaims the man,
And they in France of the best rank and station
Are most select and generous, chief in that.
Neither a borrower, nor a lender be ;
For loan oft loses both itself and friend,
And borrowing dulls the edge of husbandry.
This above all : to thine own self be true,
And it must follow, as the night the day,
Thou canst not then be false to any man.

Act I, Sc. 3

SOLILOQUY ON LIFE AND DEATH

To be, or not to be : that is the question :
Whether 'tis nobler in the mind to suffer
The slings and arrows of outrageous fortune,
Or to take arms against a sea of troubles,
And by opposing end them ? To die : to sleep ;
No more ; and, by a sleep to say we end
The heart-ache and the thousand natural shocks
That flesh is heir to, 'tis a consummation
Devoutly to be wish'd. To die, to sleep ;
To sleep : perchance to dream : ay, there's the
rub ;
For in that sleep of death what dreams may
come
When we have shuffled off this mortal coil,
Must give us pause. There's the respect
That makes calamity of so long life ;
For who would bear the whips and scorns of
time,
The oppressor's wrong, the proud man's con-
tumely,
The pangs of dispriz'd love, the law's delay,
The insolence of office, and the spurns
That patient merit of the unworthy takes,
When he himself might his quietus make
With a bare bodkin ? who would fardels bear,

To grunt and sweat under a weary life,
But that the dread of something after death,
The undiscover'd country from whose bourn
No traveller returns, puzzles the will,
And makes us rather bear those ills we have
Than fly to others that we know not of?
Thus conscience does make cowards of us all;
And thus the native hue of resolution
Is sicklied o'er with the pale cast of thought,
And enterprises of great pith and moment
With this regard their currents turn awry,
And lose the name of action.

Act 3, Sc. 1.

REFLECTIONS ON MAN

I have of late,—but wherefore I know not,—lost all my mirth, forgone all custom of exercises; and indeed it goes so heavily with my disposition that this goodly frame, the earth, seems to me a sterile promontory ; this most excellent canopy, the air, look you, this brave o'erhanging firmament, this majestical roof fretted with golden fire, why, it appears no other thing to me but a foul and pestilent congregation of vapours. What a piece of work is a man ! How noble in reason ! how infinite in faculty ! in form, in moving, how express and admirable ! in action how like an angel ! in apprehension how like a god ! the beauty of the world ! the paragon of animals ! And yet, to me, what is this quintessence of dust ? man delights not me ; no, nor woman neither, though, by your smiling, you seem to say so.

Act 2, Sc. 2.

OPHELIA'S DEATH

There is a willow grows aslant a brook,
That shows his hoar leaves in the glassy stream ;
There with fantastic garlands did she come,
Of crow-flowers, nettles, daisies, and long
purples,
That liberal shepherds give a grosser name,
But our cold maids do dead men's fingers call
them :
There, on the pendent boughs her coronet weeds
Clambering to hang, an envious sliver broke,
When down her weedy trophies and herself
Fell in the weeping brook. Her clothes spread
wide,
And, mermaid-like, awhile they bore her up ;
Which time she chanted snatches of old tunes,
As one incapable of her own distress,
Or like a creature native and indu'd
Unto that element ; but long it could not be
Till that her garments, heavy with their drink,
Pull'd the poor wretch from her melodious lay
To muddy death.

Act 4. Sc. 7.

ALAS! POOR YORICK

Alas ! poor Yorick. I knew him, Horatio ; a fellow of infinite jest, of most excellent fancy ; he hath borne me on his back a thousand times ; and now, how abhorred in my imagination it is ! my gorge rises at it. Here hung those lips that I have kissed I know not how oft. Where be your gibes now ? your gambols ? your songs ? your flashes of merriment, that were wont to set the table on a roar ? Not one now, to mock your own grinning ? quite chapfallen ? Now get you to my lady's chamber, and tell her, let her paint an inch thick, to this favour she must come ; make her laugh at that.

Act 5, Sc. 1.

LEAR IN THE STORM

Blow, winds, and crack your cheeks! rage!
  blow!
You cataracts and hurricanoes, spout
Till you have drench'd our steeples, drown'd
  the cocks!
You sulphurous and thought-executing fires,
Vaunt-couriers to oak-cleaving thunderbolts,
Singe my white head! And thou, all-shaking
  thunder,
Strike flat the thick rotundity o' the world!
Crack nature's moulds, all germens spill at once
That make ingrateful man!

Act 3, Sc. 2.

. . . . .

Poor naked wretches, whereso'er you are,
That bide the pelting of this pitiless storm,
How shall your houseless heads and unfed sides,
Your loop'd and window'd raggedness, defend
  you
From seasons such as these? O! I have ta'en
Too little care of this. Take physic, pomp;
Expose thyself to feel what wretches feel,
That thou mayest shake the superflux to them,
And show the heavens more just.

Act 3, Sc. 4.

PATIENCE AND SORROW

Patience and sorrow strove
Who should express her goodliest. You have seen
Sunshine and rain at once; her smiles and tears
Were like a better way; those happy smilets
That play'd on her ripe lip seem'd not to know
What guests were in her eyes; which parted thence,
As pearls from diamonds dropp'd. In brief,
Sorrow would be a rarity most belov'd,
If all could so become it.

Act 4, Sc. 3.

DOVER CLIFF

How fearful
And dizzy 'tis to cast one's eyes so low !
The crows and choughs that wing the midway air
Show scarce so gross as beetles ; half way down
Hangs one that gathers samphire, dreadful trade !
Methinks he seems no bigger than his head.
The fishermen that walk upon the beach
Appear like mice, and yond tall anchoring bark
Diminish'd to her cock, her cock a buoy
Almost too small for sight. The murmuring surge,
That on the unnumber'd idle pebbles chafes,
Cannot be heard so high. I'll look no more,
Lest my brain turn, and the deficient sight
Topple down headlong.

Act 4, Sc. 6.

LEAR TO CORDELIA

No, no, no, no ! Come, let's away to prison ;
We two alone will sing like birds i' the cage :
When thou dost ask me blessing, I'll kneel down,
And ask of thee forgiveness : so we'll live,
And pray, and sing, and tell old tales, and laugh
At gilded butterflies, and hear poor rogues
Talk of court news ; and we'll talk with them
too,
Who loses and who wins ; who's in, who's out ;
And take upon's the mystery of things,
As if we were God's spies : and we'll wear out,
In a wall'd prison, packs and sets of great ones
That ebb and flow by the moon.

Act 5, Sc. 3.

PERFECT CONTENT

O my soul's joy !
If after every tempest come such calms,
May the winds blow till they have waken'd
death !
And let the labouring bark climb hills of seas
Olympus-high, and duck again as low
As hell's from heaven ! If it were now to die,
'Twere now to be most happy, for I fear
My soul hath her content so absolute
That not another comfort like to this
Succeeds in unknown fate.

Act 2, Sc. 1.

REPUTATION

Good name in man and woman, dear my lord,
Is the immediate jewel of their souls :
Who steals my purse steals trash ; 'tis something, nothing ;
'Twas mine, 'tis his, and has been slave to thousands ;
But he that filches from me my good name
Robs me of that which not enriches him,
And makes me poor indeed.

Act 3, Sc. 3.

OTHELLO AND DESDEMONA

Had it pleas'd heaven
To try me with affliction, had he rain'd
All kinds of sores, and shames, on my bare head,
Steep'd me in poverty to the very lips,
Given to captivity me and my utmost hopes,
I should have found in some part of my soul
A drop of patience ; but, alas ! to make me
The fixed figure for the time of scorn
To point his slow and moving finger at ;
Yet could I bear that too ; well, very well.
But there, where I have garner'd up my heart,
Where either I must live or bear no life,
The fountain from the which my current runs
Or else dries up ; to be discarded thence !
Or keep it as a cistern for foul toads
To knot and gender in ! Turn thy complexion
there,
Patience, thou young and rose-lipp'd cherubin ;
Ay, there, look grim as hell !

Act 4, Sc. 2.

. . . . .

It is the cause, it is the cause, my soul ;
Let me not name it to you, you chaste stars !

It is the cause. Yet I'll not shed her blood,
Nor scar that whiter skin of hers than snow,
And smooth as monumental alabaster.
Yet she must die, else she'll betray more men.
Put out the light, and then put out the light :
If I quench thee, thou flaming minister,
I can again thy former light restore,
Should I repent me ; but once put out thy light,
Thou cunning'st pattern of excelling nature,
I know not where is that Promethean heat
That can thy light relume. When I have pluck'd
the rose,
I cannot give it vital growth again,
It needs must wither : I'll smell it on the tree.
[*Kisses her.*
O balmy breath, that dost almost persuade
Justice to break her sword ! One more, one
more.
Be thus when thou art dead, and I will kill thee,
And love thee after. One more, and this the
last :
So sweet was ne'er so fatal. I must weep.

Act 5, Sc. 2.

OTHELLO'S VALEDICTION

Soft you ; a word or two before you go.
I have done the state some service, and they know't ;
No more of that. I pray you, in your letters,
When you shall these unlucky deeds relate,
Speak of me as I am ; nothing extenuate,
Nor set down aught in malice : then, must you speak
Of one that lov'd not wisely but too well.

Act 5, Sc. 2.

CLEOPATRA

Age cannot wither her, nor custom stale
Her infinite variety ; other women cloy
The appetites they feed, but she makes hungry
Where most she satisfies ; for vilest things
Become themselves in her, that the holy priests
Bless her when she is riggish.

. . . .

The barge she sat in, like a burnish'd throne,
Burn'd on the water ; the poop was beaten gold,
Purple the sails, and so perfumed, that
The winds were love-sick with them, the oars were silver,
Which to the tune of flutes kept stroke, and made
The water which they beat to follow faster,
As amorous of their strokes. For her own person,
It beggar'd all description ; she did lie
In her pavilion,—cloth-of-gold of tissue,—
O'er-picturing that Venus where we see
The fancy outwork nature ; on each side her
Stood pretty-dimpled boys, like smiling Cupids,
With divers-colour'd fans, whose wind did seem
To glow the delicate cheeks which they did cool,
And what they undid did.

Act 2, Sc. 2.

MORNING SONG

Hark ! hark ! the lark at heaven's gate sings,
And Phœbus 'gins arise,
His steeds to water at those springs
On chaliced flowers that lies ;
And winking Mary-buds begin
To ope their golden eyes ;
With every thing that pretty is,
My lady sweet, arise ;
Arise, arise !

Act 2, Sc. 3.

FEAR NO MORE

Fear no more the heat o' the sun
  Nor the furious winter's rages ;
Thou thy worldly task hast done,
  Home art gone and ta'en thy wages :
Golden lads and girls all must,
As chimney-sweepers, come to dust.

Fear no more the frown o' the great,
  Thou art past the tyrant's stroke ;
Care no more to clothe and eat ;
  To thee the reed is as the oak :
The sceptre, learning, physic, must
All follow this, and come to dust.

Fear no more the lightning-flash
  Nor the all-dreaded thunder-stone ;
Fear not slander, censure rash ;
  Thou hast finished joy and moan :
All lovers young, all lovers must
Consign to thee, and come to dust.

Act 4, Sc. 2.

AGE AND YOUTH

Crabbèd Age and Youth
Cannot live together :
Youth is full of pleasance,
Age is full of care ;
Youth like summer morn,
Age like winter weather ;
Youth like summer brave,
Age like winter bare :
Youth is full of sport,
Age's breath is short ;
Youth is nimble, Age is lame :
Youth is hot and bold,
Age is weak and cold ;
Youth is wild, and Age is tame :—
Age, I do abhor thee,
Youth, I do adore thee.
O ! my love, my love is young !
Age, I do defy thee—
O sweet shepherd, hie thee,
For methinks thou stay'st too long.

From *The Passionate Pilgrim.*

AGE

When my love swears that she is made of truth,
I do believe her, though I know she lies,
That she might think me some untutor'd youth,
Unskilful in the world's false forgeries.
Thus vainly thinking that she thinks me young,
Although I know my years be past the best,
I smiling credit her false-speaking tongue,
Outfacing faults in love with love's ill rest.
But wherefore says my love that she is young?
And wherefore say not I that I am old?
O! love's best habit is a soothing tongue,
And age, in love, loves not to have years told.
Therefore I'll lie with love, and love with me,
Since that our faults in love thus smother'd be.

From *The Passionate Pilgrim.*

SUMMER'S DISTILLATION

Those hours, that with gentle work did frame
The lovely gaze where every eye doth dwell,
Will play the tyrants to the very same
And that unfair which fairly doth excel ;
For never-resting time leads summer on
To hideous winter, and confounds him there ;
Sap check'd with frost, and lusty leaves quite
    gone,
Beauty o'ersnow'd and bareness every where :
Then, were not summer's distillation left,
A liquid prisoner pent in walls of glass,
Beauty's effect with beauty were bereft,
Nor it, nor no remembrance what it was :
  But flowers distill'd, though they with winter
    meet,
  Leese but their show ; their substance still
    lives sweet.

INEXORABLE TIME

When I consider every thing that grows
Holds in perfection but a little moment,
That this huge stage presenteth nought but shows
Whereon the stars in secret influence comment ;
When I perceive that men as plants increase,
Cheered and check'd e'en by the self-same sky,
Vaunt in their youthful sap, at height decrease,
And wear their brave state out of memory ;
Then the conceit of this inconstant stay
Sets you most rich in youth before my sight,
Where wasteful Time debateth with Decay,
To change your day of youth to sullied night ;
And, all in war with Time for love of you,
As he takes from you, I engraft you new.

ETERNAL SUMMER

Shall I compare thee to a summer's day?
Thou art more lovely and more temperate;
Rough winds do shake the darling buds of May,
And summer's lease hath all too short a date:
Sometimes too hot the eye of heaven shines,
And often is his gold complexion dimmed:
And every fair from fair sometime declines,
By chance, or nature's changing course, untrimmed:
But thy eternal summer shall not fade
Nor lose possession of that fair thou owest;
Nor shall Death brag thou wanderest in his shade
When in eternal lines to time thou growest.
So long as men can breathe, or eyes can see
So long lives this, and this gives life to thee.

FORTUNE AND MEN'S EYES

When in disgrace with fortune and men's eyes
I all alone beweep my outcast state,
And trouble deaf heaven with my bootless cries,
And look upon myself, and curse my fate ;
Wishing me like to one more rich in hope,
Featured like him, like him with friends possest,
Desiring this man's art, and that man's scope,
With what I most enjoy contented least ;
Yet in these thoughts myself almost despising,
Haply I think on thee—and then my state,
Like to the lark at break of day arising
From sullen earth, sings hymns at heaven's
gate ;
For thy sweet love remembered, such wealth
brings
That then I scorn to change my state with kings.

REMEMBRANCE OF THINGS PAST

When to the sessions of sweet silent thought
I summon up remembrance of things past,
I sigh the lack of many a thing I sought,
And with old woes new wail my dear time's waste;
Then can I drown an eye, unused to flow,
For precious friends hid in death's dateless night,
And weep afresh love's long-since-cancelled woe,
And moan the expense of many a vanished sight.
Then can I grieve at grievances foregone,
And heavily from woe to woe tell o'er
The sad account of fore-bemoanèd moan,
Which I new pay as if not paid before.
--But if the while I think on thee, dear friend,
All losses are restored, and sorrows end.

THESE LINES

If Thou survive my well-contented day
When that churl Death my bones with dust
shall cover.
And shalt by fortune once more re-survey
These poor rude lines of thy deceasèd lover ;
Compare them with the bettering of the time,
And though they be outstripped by every pen,
Reserve them for my love, not for their rhyme
Exceeded by the height of happier men.
O then vouchsafe me but this loving thought—
"Had my friend's muse grown with this growing
age,
A dearer birth than this his love had brought,
To march in ranks of better equipage ;
But since he died, and poets better prove,
Theirs for their style I'll read, his for his love."

SUNS AND CLOUDS

Full many a glorious morning have I seen
Flatter the mountain-tops with sovereign eye,
Kissing with golden face the meadows green,
Gilding pale streams with heavenly alchemy ;
Anon permit the basest clouds to ride
With ugly rack on his celestial face,
And from the forlorn world his visage hide,
Stealing unseen to west with this disgrace.
Even so my sun one early morn did shine
With all-triumphant splendour on my brow ;
But out, alack ! he was but one hour mine,
The region cloud hath masked him from me
now.
Yet him for this my love no whit disdaineth ;
Suns of the world may stain when heaven's sun
staineth.

THE SOUL OF BEAUTY

O! how much more doth beauty beauteous seem
By that sweet ornament which truth doth give!
The rose looks fair, but fairer we it deem
For that sweet odour which doth in it live.
The canker-blooms have full as deep a dye
As the perfumed tincture of the roses,
Hang on such thorns, and play as wantonly
When summer's breath their masked buds discloses:
But, for their virtue only is their show,
They live unwoo'd, and unrespected fade;
Die to themselves. Sweet roses do not so;
Of their sweet deaths are sweetest odours made:
And so of you, beauteous and lovely youth,
When that shall vade, my verse distils your truth.

TIME

Like as the waves make towards the pebbled
shore,
So do our minutes hasten to their end ;
Each changing place with that which goes
before,
In sequent toil all forwards do contend.
Nativity, once in the main of light,
Crawls to maturity, wherewith being crowned,
Crooked eclipses 'gainst his glory fight,
And Time that gave, doth now his gift con-
found.
Time doth transfix the flourish set on youth,
And delves the parallels in beauty's brow ;
Feeds on the rarities of nature's truth,
And nothing stands but for his scythe to mow:—
And yet, to times in hope, my verse shall stand
Praising Thy worth, despite his cruel hand.

TWILIGHT OF LOVE

That time of year thou may'st in me behold
When yellow leaves, or none, or few, do hang
Upon those boughs which shake against the
 cold—
Bare ruined choirs, where late the sweet birds
 sang.
In me thou seest the twilight of such day
As after sunset fadeth in the west,
Which by-and-by black night doth take away,
Death's second self, that seals up all in rest :
In me thou seest the glowing of such fire
That on the ashes of his youth doth lie,
As the death-bed whereon it must expire,
Consumed with that which it was nourished by.
This thou perceiv'st, which makes thy love
 more strong,
To love that well which thou must leave ere
 long.

FAREWELL

Farewell ! thou art too dear for my possessing,
And like enough thou know'st thy estimate :
The charter of thy worth gives thee releasing ;
My bonds in thee are all determinate.
For how do I hold thee but by thy granting ?
And for that riches where is my deserving ?
The cause of this fair gift in me is wanting,
And so my patent back again is swerving.
Thyself thou gav'st, thy own worth then not
knowing,
Or me, to whom thou gav'st it, else mistaking ;
So thy great gift, upon misprision growing,
Comes home again, on better judgment making.
Thus have I had thee as a dream doth flatter,
In sleep, a king ; but waking, no such matter.

LILIES THAT FESTER

They that have power to hurt, and will do
none,
That do not do the thing they most do show,
Who, moving others, are themselves as stone,
Unmovèd, cold, and to temptation slow,—
They rightly do inherit heaven's graces,
And husband nature's riches from expense ;
They are the lords and owners of their faces,
Others, but stewards of their excellence.
The summer's flower is to the summer sweet
Though to itself it only live and die ;
But if that flower with base infection meet,
The basest weed outbraves his dignity :
For sweetest things turn sourest by their deeds ;
Lilies that fester smell far worse than weeds.

ABSENCE

From you have I been absent in the spring,
When proud-pied April, dress'd in all his trim,
Hath put a spirit of youth in every thing,
That heavy Saturn laugh'd and leap'd with him.
Yet nor the lays of birds, nor the sweet smell
Of different flowers in odour and in hue,
Could make me any summer's story tell,
Or from their proud lap pluck them where they grew :
Nor did I wonder at the lily's white,
Nor praise the deep vermilion in the rose ;
They were but sweet, but figures of delight,
Drawn after you, you pattern of all those.
Yet seem'd it winter still, and, you away,
As with your shadow I with these did play.

CHRONICLE OF WASTED TIME

When in the chronicle of wasted time
I see descriptions of the fairest wights,
And beauty making beautiful old rhyme
In praise of ladies dead, and lovely knights ;
Then in the blazon of sweet beauty's best
Of hand, of foot, of lip, of eye, of brow,
I see their antique pen would have exprest
Ev'n such a beauty as you master now.
So all their praises are but prophecies
Of this our time, all, you prefiguring ;
And for they looked but with divining eyes,
They had not skill enough your worth to sing !
For we, which now behold these present days,
Have eyes to wonder, but lack tongues to praise.

LOVE IS NOT LOVE WHICH ALTERS

Let me not to the marriage of true minds
Admit impediments. Love is not love
Which alters when it alteration finds,
Or bends with the remover to remove :—
O no ! it is an ever-fixèd mark
That looks on tempests, and is never shaken ;
It is the star to every wandering bark,
Whose worth's unknown, although his height
be taken.
Love's not Time's fool, though rosy lips and
cheeks
Within his bending sickle's compass come :
Love alters not with his brief hours and weeks,
But bears it out ev'n to the edge of doom.
If this be error, and upon me proved,
I never writ, nor no man ever loved.

DESPITE TIME

No, Time, thou shalt not boast that I do change:
Thy pyramids built up with newer might,
To me are nothing novel, nothing strange ;
They are but dressings of a former sight.
Our dates are brief, and therefore we admire
What thou dost foist upon us that is old,
And rather make them born to our desire
Than think that we before have heard them
told.
Thy registers and thee I both defy,
Not wondering at the present nor the past ;
For thy records and what we see do lie,
Made more or less by thy continual haste.
This I do vow, and this shall ever be,
I will be true, despite thy scythe and thee.

BODY AND SOUL

Poor Soul, the centre of my sinful earth,
Fooled by those rebel powers that thee array,
Why dost thou pine within, and suffer dearth,
Painting thy outward walls so costly gay?
Why so large cost, having so short a lease,
Dost thou upon thy fading mansion spend?
Shall worms, inheritors of this excess,
Eat up thy charge? is this thy body's end?
Then, Soul, live thou upon thy servant's loss,
And let that pine to aggravate thy store;
Buy terms divine in selling hours of dross;
Within be fed, without be rich no more:—
So shalt thou feed on Death, that feeds on men,
And Death once dead, there's no more dying
then.

THE PHŒNIX AND TURTLE

Let the bird of loudest lay,
On the sole Arabian tree,
Herald sad and trumpet be,
To whose sound chaste wings obey.

But thou shrieking harbinger,
Foul precurrer of the fiend,
Augur of the fever's end,
To this troop come thou not near.

From this session interdict
Every fowl of tyrant wing,
Save the eagle, feather'd king:
Keep the obsequy so strict.

Let the priest in surplice white
That defunctive music can,
Be the death-divining swan,
Lest the requiem lack his right.

And thou treble-dated crow,
That thy sable gender mak'st
With the breath thou giv'st and tak'st,
'Mongst our mourners shalt thou go.

Here the anthem doth commence :
Love and constancy is dead ;
Phœnix and the turtle fled
In a mutual flame from hence.

So they lov'd, as love in twain
Had the essence but in one ;
Two distincts, division none :
Number there in love was slain.

Hearts remote, yet not asunder ;
Distance, and no space was seen
'Twixt the turtle and his queen :
But in them it were a wonder.

So between them love did shine,
That the turtle saw his right
Flaming in the phœnix' sight ;
Either was the other's mine.

Property was thus appall'd,
That the self was not the same ;
Single nature's double name
Neither two nor one was call'd.

Reason, in itself confounded,
Saw division grow together ;
To themselves yet either neither,
Simple were so well compounded,

That it cried, " How true a twain
Seemeth this concordant one !
Love hath reason, reason none,
If what parts can so remain."

Whereupon it made this threne
To the phœnix and the dove,
Co-supremes and stars of love,
As chorus to their tragic scene.

THRENOS

Beauty, truth, and rarity,
Grace in all simplicity,
Here enclos'd in cinders lie.

Death is now the phœnix' nest ;
And the turtle's loyal breast
To eternity doth rest,

Leaving no posterity :
'Twas not their infirmity,
It was married chastity.

Truth may seem, but cannot be ;
Beauty brag, but 'tis not she ;
Truth and beauty buried be.

To this urn let those repair
That are either true or fair ;
For these dead birds sigh a prayer.

CARLYLE ON SHAKESPEARE

IF I say, therefore, that Shakespeare's is the greatest of Intellects, I have said all concerning him. But there is more in Shakespeare's intellect than we have yet seen. It is what I call an unconscious intellect; there is more virtue in it than he himself is aware of. Novalis beautifully remarks of him, that those Dramas of his are Products of Nature too, deep as Nature herself. I find a great truth in this saying. Shakespeare's Art is not Artifice; the noblest worth of it is not there by plan or precontrivance. It grows-up from the deeps of Nature, through this noble sincere soul who is a voice of Nature. The latest generations of men will find new meanings in Shakespeare, new elucidations of their own human being; "new harmonies with the infinite structure of the Universe; concurrences with later ideas, affinities with the higher powers and senses of man." This well deserves meditating. It is Nature's highest reward to a true simple great soul, that he get thus to be *a part of herself*. Such a man's works, whatsoever he with utmost conscious exertion of forethought shall accomplish, grow up withal *un*consciously, from the unknown deeps in him—as the oak-tree grows from the Earth's bosom, as the mountains and waters shape themselves ; with a symmetry grounded on Nature's own laws, comformable to all Truth whatsoever. How much in Shakespeare lies hid ; his sorrows, his silent struggles known to himself ; much that was not known at all, not speakable at all ; like *roots*, like sap and forces working underground ! Speech is great ; but Silence is greater.

Heroes and Hero-Worship